SIGNATURES

OF

GRACE

With Essays by

MURRAY BODO, O.F.M.

ANDRE DUBUS

MARY GORDON

PATRICIA HAMPL

RON HANSEN

PAULA HUSTON

PAUL MARIANI

KATHERINE VAZ

SIGNATURES

OF

GRACE

*Catholic Writers
on the Sacraments*

Edited by
THOMAS GRADY
and PAULA HUSTON

A DUTTON BOOK

DUTTON
Published by the Penguin Group
Penguin Putnam Inc., 375 Hudson Street, New York, New York 10014, U.S.A.
Penguin Books Ltd, 27 Wrights Lane, London W8 5TZ, England
Penguin Books Australia Ltd, Ringwood, Victoria, Australia
Penguin Books Canada Ltd, 10 Alcorn Avenue, Toronto, Ontario, Canada M4V 3B2
Penguin Books (N.Z.) Ltd, 182–190 Wairau Road, Auckland 10, New Zealand

Penguin Books Ltd, Registered Offices: Harmondsworth, Middlesex, England

First published by Dutton, a member of Penguin Putnam Inc.

First Printing, March, 2000
10 9 8 7 6 5 4 3 2 1

LIBRARY OF CONGRESS CATALOGING-IN-PUBLICATION DATA
Signatures of grace : Catholic writers on the sacraments / edited by Thomas Grady
and Paula Huston.
p.   cm.
ISBN 0-525-94533-4
1. Sacraments—Catholic Church.   I. Grady, Thomas (Thomas R.)   II. Huston,
Paula.
BX2200 .S47   2000
234'.16—dc21   99-057412

Printed in the United States of America
Set in Centaur
Designed by Eve L. Kirch

To the monks of the New Camaldoli Hermitage,
Big Sur, California, and
Marmion Abbey, Aurora, Illinois

CONTENTS

Preface   ix

1. Baptism   *Katherine Vaz*   I

2. Penance   *Patricia Hampl*   34

3. Eucharist   *Ron Hansen*   69

4. Confirmation   *Paul Mariani*   98

5. Matrimony   *Paula Huston*   131

6. Holy Orders   *Murray Bodo, O.F.M.*   164

7. Anointing of the Sick   *Mary Gordon*   193

Epilogue: Sacraments   *Andre Dubus*   220

About the Contributors   233

PREFACE

Signatures of Grace began to take shape in the first few hours of our meeting at a writers' conference along the central California coast just two years ago. After spending some time in agreeable shoptalk, the two of us, a novelist and an editor, quite accidentally discovered that serious Catholics lurked below the surface. The trajectories of our professional lives had brought us together at the conference—one of us a lifelong Catholic schooled by Benedictines, the other a recent convert who had spent some formative time at a Camaldolese hermitage just up the road at Big Sur—and within a few months, the idea for this volume of essays on the sacraments by contemporary Catholic writers had been born and its earliest contributors had enthusiastically agreed to participate.

This enthusiasm, in retrospect, is not hard to understand. Sacraments, according to the old three-part catechism formulation, are "outward signs instituted by Christ to give grace," and while the history of the instituting and the precise work of the grace are perhaps the provinces of a church historian or a theologian, who better than a novelist or a poet to help us understand the experience of these "signs," each of which is associated with such earthy realities as water, oil, bread, and wine? So it was that Katherine Vaz, a swimmer, chose to write about the water of Baptism; Mary Gordon warmed to the sensuous nature of the chrism used in the Anointing of the Sick; and Ron Hansen recalled the feel of the Communion wafer on the roof of his mouth. The purely *aesthetic* experience of the sacraments—arguably the most distinctive feature of Catholic life—is at least one source of their appeal to our imaginations.

Beyond the visible signs, though, are the invisible, spiritual realities to which they point. Each is, as Mary Gordon puts it, "a vehicle for the journey between the seen and the unseen." The Roman Catholic church recognizes seven such signs as sacraments, and the common way of clustering them is as Sacraments of Initiation (Baptism, Eucharist, Confirmation), Sacraments of Healing (Penance, Anointing of the Sick), and Sacraments at the Service of Communion (Matrimony, Holy Orders). We have chosen, however, to arrange the essays in this volume in the order in which the sacraments might be received. Each marks one of the spiritual milestones of the great human journey: birth, the joining of lives in commitment, the dedication of a life to religious service, death.

From the first, we were determined that the essays in this volume be written expressly for it so that each contribution would be sure to cover, albeit in different ways, the same ground: the history and meaning of the sacrament as well as the writer's experience with it. Only the late Andre Dubus's essay on the sacramentality of everyday life, which serves as an epilogue here, has appeared before in print. That essay poignantly describes what has been called a sacramental vision of life—the possibility that grace might attend, even unexpectedly burst in upon, the least of our doings. Such is the mystery, in Katherine Vaz's lovely phrase, of how "sacramental rites wait to be replicated in our quotidian lives" or how, as Father Murray Bodo puts it, "all of creation is an immense sacrament."

Just how or even when this attendant grace might "work" turns out to be difficult to explain precisely or even detect at all. Ron Hansen, for example, confides that after making his first Communion, there was "no hint that I was under new management." Paul Mariani records what seems to be the impact of his own Confirmation, a moment when "the Spirit had conspired to dissolve time itself"—although that experience took place long after the actual sacramental rite. All of us involved in the making of this book, in fact, have discovered unexpected ways in which the signs of water, oil, bread, and wine have changed our lives. But finally, each writer, in his or her own way, acknowledges the mystery that is at the heart of every sacramental transaction, the conclusion that Patricia Hampl comes to: "You don't get to understand; you just get to acquiesce."

We are immensely grateful to our contributors. Quite by accident we have managed to present a sampling of the diversity of American Catholicism. Paul Mariani and Mary Gordon invoke the world of East Coast Irish and Italian Catholicism. Katherine Vaz, a Portuguese American, was raised in California. Ron Hansen (Nebraska) and Patricia Hampl (Minnesota) draw on the hearty German, Irish, and Czech Catholicism of the Midwest. Father Murray Bodo grew up in New Mexico. Andre Dubus's roots were in the French Catholicism of Louisiana. Thanks to all of them for the care and devotion that so clearly emanates from their work.

Tom offers his warm thanks to his wife, Mary, and to their children, Michael and Maggie, for the continuous grace of their love and support. Paula wishes to thank her husband, Mike, and their children, Andrea, Johnny, Kelly, and Greta, for all the joy they have given her over the years. We both wish to thank Clare Ferraro, Philip Higgs, Robin Levine, Cindy Achar, Arthur Maisel, and Juliette St. Jacques at Dutton for their enthusiasm, help, and encouragement.

SIGNATURES

OF

GRACE

Baptism

KATHERINE VAZ

To celebrate my Baptism, my grandmother tried to pierce my ears. I was her first granddaughter, and she wanted my flesh imbedded with the gold earrings she had worn as a baby, the ones she must have been saving for precisely this moment. She put a cork behind one of my earlobes to arrest any shock conveyed by the point of the threaded needle. Inches from stitching me to her heart's wish, she felt my mother grab her arm. My Vó had not bothered to ask for permission, perhaps because she knew it would not be given.

Of course I remember none of this. Baptism highlights a basic mystery: Our own first chapters will remain beyond our memories, locked into silence. We search for stories and immersions for the rest of our lives. I have to imagine myself on display in my crib, which was set out on the confetti-style gold-flecked linoleum that everyone bought in the fifties to hide the dirt. Kicking and spewing with the colic I was told afflicted me until I was weaned onto goat's milk, I no doubt fussed my way through being the featured event at Our Lady of Grace Church in Castro Valley, east of San Francisco. Father Pruitt, handsome enough for my mother and her friends to refer to him as a "what-a-waste priest," used words and water—fundamentals of ordinary human life—to impart a seal that would make me forever receptive to supernatural grace.

I was wearing the Irish lace baptismal gown, silk-lined, that my mother's parents bought on their honeymoon in Paris in 1920. My mother wore it, and her six children would take their turns, followed by my seven nieces and nephews. The silk lining has long since sloughed its particles into the air, which prompts me to think less about continuity and more about Baptism being called an invitation to write our own epics: Links to the past are frightfully tenuous. I admire this sacrament's tendency to be beyond our consciousness, since we are charged from birth with the task of translating the unknown into the known, of making silence speak, of sending our imaginations in search of the truth. I was born in earthquake country, and therefore I paint into the scene some roses bright from the minerals churning in the land.

Making silence speak.

How do I go beyond memory to find my father's mother after she attempted to give me her heirloom earrings, to pierce me with love? Possibly she went into the kitchen and scrubbed dishes. Silence and loudly running water. In my bodily tissue, fragile as wet paper, without knowing it, I was already writing down that somehow I had managed to disappoint her from the start.

Her name was Maria de Amparo Serpa Vaz, but she preferred to be called Mary. She was born in Angra do Heroísmo, the capital of Terceira in the Azores. The ocean air around the islands is said to swarm with the voices of drowned fishermen and pirates; the water and words are joined into a death-filled, living reverberation, pounding beyond the audible. She came from a fiery place and a fierce family. (Her aunt once knocked down a bayonet-waving soldier in order to bring bread into a village under quarantine.) How had fate tied her to such a goggle-eyed, mute changeling like me?

I grew up into a quiet child, though my head swam with words, a white-water rush. Sometimes the spume of them left a froth that I could see in my mind after the words had passed. For the life of me, I could not figure how to grasp a sentence out of that fast-running current to answer a simple question put to me. When I was older and read Maxine Hong Kingston's *The Woman Warrior*, about a Chinese girl in Stockton whose classmates gang up to scream, "Speak! Say something!" while the tears run down her face and still, still she cannot utter a reply, I at last realized that I was far from being alone.

I had a pronounced fear of doing or saying anything that might lead to a confrontation—that is, to an acute awareness of myself as a physical being. Vó spoke Portuguese but had to learn English, and the studious avoidance of mistakes must have struck her as a distasteful luxury. Sometimes, though, at family parties, she tied up my hair with a ribbon from a gift box, and I sat like a surprise package on her lap, as if she were waiting for permission to open me. This silence I read as love so fragile that words would have marred it.

When I was twelve, I noticed that certain truths, plain or melodic, could only be expressed in the written word. Writers tapped into the wellspring that everyone carried around but never got to use in everyday speech. I would not write to say what I thought, but to invite everything I did not know. I was happy to dive inside myself but longed to plunge into the world in some fluid but literal way, which translated itself into the launching of my lifelong affection for swimming. Every day in summer, my sister Maria and I jumped into the pool at Castro Valley High. I moved in larky configurations with other people, arms and legs weightless, silence enriched with a flow of shapes and shades, as if we were darting inside a painting. When I leapt from the high dive, the finger of a stretching, invisible glove caught me in blueness, lucid and tactile, yet pleasingly blurred, like the double vision when I took off my glasses on land. We were fearless. Maria and I kicked anyone who tried to drown us. I inhaled the hormonal top notes perfuming everyone's skin. One can assemble a down-to-earth Baptism anywhere: under the spray of water, with the throb of the physical below mystery's drape.

But eventually I had to return to the surface, where Vó's passion for tidiness was increasing. When leaves scuttled like little monkeys' paws over the walkway near her apartment, she slammed them into the trash. She hung towels over the plastic bags covering her clothing, and once a week she laundered the towels. She scoured enough to wear down metal and dusted until I realized that hers was the only place I had seen where no motes danced in the light. Ramparts of pure air entered where she was.

I was another project and needed fattening up. Imprisoned at her kitchen table, I faced platters of fried chicken while portraits of Jesus and the Pope stared down. A river of soprano notes flooded in from the two dozen canaries she kept in the huge cage outside. These birds were lime, orange, and the color that children use to depict the sun, and their music poured through her immaculate rooms and onto busy East 14th Street, past Pring's Restaurant with its neon chicken dressed in chaps. I sat caught in this river between the garish bird and the beautiful ones, but this rapturous tension did not save me. Vó said, "You eat like a bird, Katherine," and rinsed the plates of whatever I rejected.

One day the firmness of her touch led to a disaster between us. At a cousin's Baptism, Vó decided that I would be lost in the sea of people outside the church if she did not clasp my hand and lead me along. I was beyond holding hands with a grown-up, and I stopped in my tracks, prying at her heavy fingers and pulling my arm to loosen her grip. Where were my parents? My memory is contracted into nothing but this tug-of-war with my grandmother. I was sick with fury that she was stronger.

She jerked me to her and leaned down to say, "I don't want to lose you." Her hat, a black veil attached to black feathers, looked like a bird's wing dipping down a net for a sea catch out of her eyes.

I offered no reply.

She would not let me go even when we were seated in the pew.

My hand sweated, trapped, inside the hand of my perpetual laundress of a grandmother while the Baptism provided its laundering service for the soul. Our Carmelite Sisters of Charity, an order airlifted out of Spain during its Civil War to settle in an unlikely California suburb, would draw hearts on the blackboard at school, fill them in with chalk, and then erase the blotted interiors to demonstrate what the sacrament sets out to do. Without this washing away of original sin, our inheritance from Adam's fall, we would be denied admission to heaven.

My baptized cousin, startled by the violent shock of cold water, screeched on the altar right as an awful notion seized me. Vó was assuming that I did not want to hold her hand because I was ashamed of her or did not love her.

I twitched in dismay and breathed out a small echo of the cry of the baptized child, and Vó read my discomfort in a reasonable way. She concluded that I was continuing to fret, and she dropped my hand.

We did not speak for the rest of the day, now terrible with the weight of her declaring, Good-bye, then; I'll let you go.

Again—again!—I was speechless with Vó the afternoon I found her weeping over a dead canary. It was the treasured one that she kept in a cage inside. They shared a formalized goodnight routine, trilling to each other before the ceremonial draping of the cage with a clean, ironed cloth. She chatted to her prized canary throughout the day, and it sang back wildly. For her it dressed up the void better than I could.

I might have run to her or embraced a sadness we could bear together, but I froze. She was embarrassed by my stance, as well as by her tears, out of proportion to the death of this minute creature. The faraway gaze she let sweep over me announced that she was crying over more than her widowhood, more than this bird, more than I knew, and more than she could express even if she could name it.

I had not yet learned her truest history. That would come much later. For now, my discovery was more general: The most precious, semi-sealed dimension of everyone else was silent, too, and overflowed to create intensifications in the silence surrounding us all. We must deal with real people in real rooms, or else "mystery" is only so much embroidered air. When I went away to college, I lacked the words to tell her that this lesson was one of her parting gifts to me.

My college roommate, Lee Haines, took everything I possessed about silence, water, and words and forced it into action. She often drove us very fast in her green Volvo sports car from our Santa Barbara apartment to the Los Angeles County Museum of Art to view the heated ridges on the impressionist paintings. She did batiks using Australian aboriginal designs; she filled notebooks with line drawings; she once undertook Japanese raku ceramic firing at the University of California kiln and spent a panicked hour extinguishing a fire she set in some nearby straw. We read books, cooked dinner for friends, went to parties. We swam in the ocean. Am I making her sound as if she rushed from one feat to the next? What my best friend taught me was slowness. A person should carefully but definitely remove the wrapping of a day and express pleasure, and then lift the day into view.

Did I want pierced ears? (Vó associated earrings with birth, but I linked them to being an adult.) Very well; Lee would take me to the nurse in the jewelry department at Nordstrom's.

I pierced my ears.

Did I want to write? Fine; I must *begin*.

My silence took a dedicated turn because of Lee. Every morning from six to nine, no matter how late I had stayed up the evening before or how assiduously I was falling in or out of love with one boy after another, I sat in one of the peach-colored study carrels in the library and copied out stories to seep inside them and see how a writer constructed the underwater bridges. I followed the tributaries in Proust, mapped the conflicts in Flaubert, studied transitions in Fitzgerald.

The baptized are often referred to as the receivers of stories, with the sacrament framing a poetry of belief. Out of this comes grace, which is often described in aquatic terms, as the thirteenth-century mystic, Mechthild of Magdeburg, put it, "a heavenly flood out of the spring of the flowing Trinity." I was pursuing a secular version of this, what Philip Larkin in his poem "Water" calls the religion he would like to invent, with "images of sousing" and a litany that employs a "furious, devout drench." For me that meant finding some marriage of water and words that referred not only to language on a page but to the living ways in which people in their bodies could happen upon wonder as they moved through the unpredictable, sensuous world. Virginia Woolf captures this in her story "Kew Gardens." Characters stroll toward the shade, and the sun melts them into patches of light and drops of color and water. These people assume a stillness unto death as they sink down, but their words have also splashed to the ground and will remain vital in the landscape.

I wrote beginner's stories and was so saturated with words, and a love of them, that useful, practical sentences ebbed out of me, letting me speak on and on with friends, with professors, with strangers.

With my grandmother. The clothing of the seventies appalled her, and she sniffed that only wealthy kids would mock the poor by wearing tatters. But when I came home and visited her, she threw her arms around me until I inhaled the bath powder off her neck. Lilacs. Soaped flesh. I hugged her back. Her black, wavy hair was now iron. I think she considered college as the future into which smart children vanished, abandoning their immigrant grandparents. When she saw my pierced ears, she released a shout of happiness and offered me some earrings.

While I put them on—gold filigree hoops—she got out a bottle of Galliano to mark the ceremony.

"Don't tell your father I'm giving you a drink," she said. She giggled, and the lilting of the outdoor canaries projected the tints of their bodies like streamers into the air around us.

"I won't."

"Promise me. This is our secret, you and me."

"I promise, Vóvó," I said. My hand rested near hers on the spotless tablecloth. She often wore neatly pressed slacks now, no more solid black but the grays worn by Portuguese widows to show they have risen beyond mourning but not quite into the levity of color.

She washed the bottle's lip, resealed it, and rinsed the sponge before setting it on a paper towel to dry. (Some things were not going to change.) Did I need her to ask Saint Anthony for some favors this week? I received good grades in college, but did I need his help with love? I admitted that I did. Every day she lit candles and knelt with her rosary and petitions for her grandchildren, and she liked giving the saint highly specific requests.

Vó and I found a torrent of words and—not exactly water. Galliano was sweeter, something much better.

Did I hear that my shy Tia Conceição had survived breaking her neck? Quiet people could be the toughest. Did I know that Mrs. Correia thought in a language of color? This skill ran in her family. Mrs. Correia could not use a telephone because numbers looked to her like fishhooks strewn on a white beach. My father dabbed different shades over the numerals on her phone dial and made a placard with pictures of the hospital, police station, and his house matched up with necklaces of seven dabs of color to replicate each phone number. Now she could dial chromatically. Mrs. Correia made shopping lists in tinted codes; I wish she had transcribed her dreams.

My godmother, Clementina, informed me that back home in the Azores, Vó had been a lively party girl, a bawdy gossip. Amazing! She never spun any illicit tales for me, and I consoled myself with the reminder that she still pictured me as the bird at her table, weak of stomach. At least now the storyteller in her wanted to coax out the storyteller in me. I volleyed back funny, censored reports of my adventures in college.

Vó would die before the deepest part of me connected to the deepest part of her. But it was my friend who first spoke to me

Baptism

out of death's wide silence. In 1980, when Lee and I were both twenty-five and I was already several years married in Los Angeles, she was diagnosed with the brain tumor that would kill her over the length of a year.

Lee underwent radiation treatments at George Washington University Hospital in Washington, D.C., and suffered an affliction called "auras." Impulses in the pit of her stomach triggered sensations in a jumble of memories that, as she wrote in her journal, "are really half-memories, because they happen too fast to register as anything remembered." Tastes—burnt corn, metal— entered her mouth, and dustbins of non sequiturs got overturned in her brain. Her right side was paralyzed; she wrote slowly with her left hand.

Her parents, Helen and Jerry, moved her back to southern California, and now and then I picked her up in my car and took her on outings. My husband was insisting that I help him in his failing catering business, and I was eager to flee whenever I could. One visit that will never leave me was when she asked if we could walk to the library for a book on Asian art; her knowledge of it was lacking. She needed a cane and leaned on my arm, but my strongest impression was that this was Lee being herself, not Lee concocting a brave final year.

When I visited her in Whittier before her surgery, we swam in her parents' pool and talked until the night chill made them call us in, a grand dissolving of words with water. When I said goodbye, she walked me to the door, though I told her not to trouble herself. "Of course I should," she said. "I need to do everything as long as I'm able."

[11]

Speech failed her after the surgery was unsuccessful. Her tongue stopped forming words. By the time I brought Lee a scarf, she was beyond caring about covering her head. When I brought chocolate at my next visit, she could not swallow. What was left for us was to sit together, no speaking possible, with me in awe at being allowed into this most intimate realm, that of a person's own dying. Her gift to me was to enclose her fears inside herself. When my death came, maybe I would resurrect this wedded physical and spiritual power of not being afraid.

She reserved a stunning tribute for her parents. Over dinner in the hospital's cafeteria, they suddenly stared at each other and raced back to her room. She was calling to them across a vast space and held on long enough for them to be at her side and say good-bye. Such a surge of grace—what a furious, devout drench of love from Lee, and from them back to her, to make silence profoundly speak.

I have a photograph of the sun pinning flowers of mild fire onto Lee's brown hair. The autumn leaves are scarlet. She is in Washington, D.C., bundled in a red-snowflake sweater. That her face tilts upward with joy is not surprising, since she is an artist in an outpouring of shades. What startles me is that when this photo was taken, she already knew about her tumor. Agony awaits; the time is even now upon her. But what a celebration, this flooding of carmine and auburn, this untamed, bloody painting of leaves, and with her so beautiful that she and her landscape do not fear anything, including suffusions of death.

Above my desk, I keep an ink drawing she made for me— "Two Guards," figures with their arms crossed and their hair rigid in fright. Although in the photograph Lee is calm, in her art-work she depicts dread, and I admire her range just as I distrust bravado incapable of sorrow. Two pictures—one of who she is temporally and the other an example of the artistic permanence we can create, if only we imagine that our life begins at once and not at some indefinable point when we decide we are prepared.

Memory deserted me when I composed a eulogy; shock erased parts of my mind. I ended up talking about us using her green car to escape. My husband did not attend the service. Death frightened him (which scared me about him), and he added that a funeral would hardly bring her back. In going by myself to join the congregation saying good-bye to Lee, I knew that I was about to plummet quite alone into much more.

While working in my husband's catering business, I spent an hour after a party picking frillpicks off a lawn. The hostess stood bossing me around, and I pretended that I was hunting Easter eggs as I found the yellow, red, and blue cellophane on the tooth-picks. Night was falling. This was a relief, not to camouflage my humiliation but because I had stopped eating—food nauseated me—and the boils now covering me caused people in daylight to stare. It looked as if my insides had exploded and were working through my skin. In the dark, I merely looked like a creature spray-painted over chicken bones.

I did not write; I quit swimming.

My marriage ended.

Dying underscores the duality of nature and spirit: Is the flesh our garrison? Or is the soul solidly who we are, rather than the body as it fulfills its obligation to fail us? Why this divide? Why did my wasting away seem inextricable from a waning of my spirit? As C. S. Lewis remarked, "We fear ghosts and dislike corpses . . . in reality we hate the division which makes possible the conception of either corpse or ghost."

Mrs. Correia, who thought in color, passed away in her sleep. My mother's mother died; I had adored her quick wit and grand-dame past as a flapper in New York. A man I met and liked stopped calling me, and then I read in the newspaper that he had died.

Vó was dying of stomach cancer when I was a floater, a divorced woman crashing on a borrowed futon and piecing together unre-markable money as a copy editor. I returned to the sense that she disapproved of me. I fumbled around asking if I could do any-thing for her, but all she wanted was to stay alive long enough for my brother's wedding. When I adjusted the bandana on her thin-ning hair, she flinched.

We did, however, manage a fond exchange. My godmother, Clementina, offered to buy me a ticket so that I would accompany her to Portugal—ocean, a language full of "shh, shh" sounds—but we were reluctant to go with Vó so ill. But Vó insisted; she wanted us to take an envelope with her photograph and a few dollars and leave it at the shrine in Fátima, where the Virgin Mary appeared to three shepherd children in 1917. We would team up in a last-ditch appeal for a miracle.

On a blazing hot anniversary of the apparition, Clementina and I pushed through the crowds to leave my grandmother's face at this nexus where the Church agreed that one world met the other.

I was back in California to see Vó on my brother's wedding day, but she was not well enough to attend. As I was leaning forward to hug her good-bye, she hurried me out of her apartment along with my parents, brothers, and sisters. What looked like cinders were lifting off her scalp, and it was this hint of ash that undid me, but she had no interest in an unkempt scene. She kissed us hastily, telling us to leave or we would be late, and shut the door. Her final comment to one of my brothers was that she disliked the suit he had chosen.

Only her sister, my Tia Conceição, stayed with her while the rest of us went to the wedding. Vó had already died when bidding us farewell, but willpower—her refusal to mar the start of a happy day with the messiness of dying—had propelled her to bustle and urge us along. After we departed, she donned her sea-dark burial dress and collapsed.

Her ability to array herself minutes away from death was haunting, because the simplest acts of willpower began to elude me. Every time I looked in my closet, a panicked inner voice said: *Just pick out a dress, take it off the hanger, and put it on.* I could not move. I didn't know that this was heartbreak. It didn't register for years that I was learning to have compassion for everyone's story, especially for the ways in which we observe ourselves and miss the obvious. The few photos of me back then in Los Angeles show a skeleton. I was learning forgiveness for people's tossed-off habit of saying, Sure, I'd love to have a nervous breakdown if I could find the time. My faithful sister Maria, living in Pasadena, came by to dress me and take me swimming with orders that I build back up, starting with one lap, and that I compose a few sentences and wait for the reservoir to refill.

At our Baptism, we were made permanently receptive to grace. But it need not arrive in one tremendous flood, cleansing away all pain. It is better to learn, slowly, how to retain a knowledge of sorrow. Grace can flow to us in increments, hardly noticed, if we cling to ways of baptizing each day. My rebirth had been cast before I was born: My father, August, offered me a lifelong example of staying routinely open to grace.

He has painted every day since he was a boy, through decades of teaching and into his retirement. When he was nineteen, he decorated his father's car tarp with a Last Judgment scene. He completed a roaring ocean during one of my screaming jags as an infant. Sometimes he stacks finished canvases so rapidly that they dry together and make kissing noises when pried apart. As an historian, he believes that any occurrence or person who ever lived coexists with us and is a worthy subject. In his variation of "Where's Waldo," for a diversion, he will wander in history and paint himself as a Brueghel-like dancing peasant or a gentleman disembarking from a train on the Barbary Coast.

One brushstroke follows another. This inventiveness, this expansiveness about time—this daily, baptismal impulse to welcome creation—must have inspired me to write one page and then another. Bad and good days dissolved into a sense of the continuous present. I published a novel about a mute girl who uses a language of color, and then I finished the research for my next book.

Joy—especially its return after a long time receded—finds

other joy. I married a man I met in water. He told me about the "language of light," the realm of the animals so far into the ocean's darkness that they speak by pulsating their phosphorescent bodies.

I became a godmother to Maria's son, Daniel Duarte, my parents' first grandchild (and later to my sister Teresa's son, Joseph). He wore the Irish lace gown. A white garment symbolizes newness; despite centuries of quarrels over Baptism's meaning, its symbols and actual ceremony are little changed since the earliest known monographs, Tertullian's *De Baptismo*, written in the year 200 in North Africa, and fifteen years later, the *Treatise on the Apostolic Tradition* by Saint Hippolytus. There has always been some form of an exorcism (disavowal of sin), a pouring of water, words, and an anointing with oil (chrism). Salt might be administered on the tongue to signify the ocean, immortality.

Thousands of candles have, over the years, burned an implacable scent of wax into the air of St. Leander's Church, the parish of my sister, her husband, Derek, and their son. Father Mangini asked me to speak for Daniel: Had he renounced evil? I replied that he had, although he was misbehaving and fussing, and I was afraid I might drop him. Maria was sighing at Daniel's loud stage manner. During the Profession of Faith, he was shrieking.

"Hey," whispered my brother Mark, "that's some farewell to old Satan."

Daniel also did not much care for the pouring of water on his head. His face went crimson. His godfather, Chris Duarte, comforted him. Daniel's memory will not retrieve this day, any more than I can recall my own Baptism, but as a godmother I could perceive how graphically this sacrament threatens to be our first consigning of ceremony to empty gesture, the spiritual equivalent of getting an inoculation. Or a ticket punched, just in case there's a gatekeeper in heaven. If Baptism causes violent upheaval by invoking divine grace, why do so many of us regard it as merely the washing away of that chalk-white heart of original sin? This conjures the specter of the Reformation, when Protestants objected that Baptism had indeed dwindled into a quasi-magical rite.

One of my father's decorated candles blazed on the altar. Daniel quieted down after Father Mangini anointed him with oil. Holding my nephew in my arms, I was dismayed at any assertion that we are born as stained creatures.

Saint Augustine played a substantial role in this emphasis upon original sin, and my father would gladly paint this historical figure, his patron saint, onto the scene as we line up for photos. Derek is one of ten children; everyone begins jostling around.

"This isn't photography," says my mother, Elizabeth, to the man with the camera. "This is crowd control."

I picture Saint Augustine's skin dried out from his years as the Bishop of Hippo on Africa's seacoast—and from his earlier career of dissipation. "Remember my famous anguished cry, 'O Lord make me pure, but not just yet?' " he murmurs to me. "I wanted the Church to be for sinners as well as saints. We're heir to flesh that's weak."

"The condition of concupiscence," my mother says. "You drove your poor mother crazy. Now pipe down and line up."

I wonder out loud about the point of being baptized as a child. Though I'm aware that it makes us receptive to grace for the rest of our lives, why not wait until we can bring that awareness to the ceremony? Adults once consciously chose faith: Lent used to be preferred for the catechumenate (phase of preparation), with Easter as the ideal day for Baptism, to be followed swiftly by Confirmation and the Eucharist. These still constitute the "sacraments of initiation."

Saint Augustine is in a fever of being misunderstood. "We're inclined to sin from birth, and we need God's grace from the beginning to combat it," he says. Besides, once the apostles started carrying out Christ's directive that Baptism was necessary for salvation, the urgency about baptizing infants was inevitable.

Into St. Leander's wanders Pelagius, the theologian who challenged Augustine by denying the existence of original sin and declaring that man was in charge of his moral fortunes and could choose not to go astray. He casts a judging eye on me; shouldn't Daniel wait until he can consent to making an act of faith? "It's up to the individual to establish himself as holy in the divine sight," he says.

"Justification," says my mother. She knows all the terms. "You keep quiet, too."

"A person must be justified, made open to grace, from the beginning, or it won't happen," Augustine insists, eyes crazed. Didn't he persuade the bishops in A.D. 416 to condemn the teachings of Pelagius? Why can't a person ever be over and done with his rivals?

Pelagius obeys my mother and assumes his place among the ghosts in the assembly. They're always present, my father would remind me. We have to imagine them there to understand the history of whatever we're doing. The photographer snaps the picture.

Pelagius cannot resist a last salvo at Augustine. "You backed yourself and the rest of us into a corner," he says. He's right. If Baptism is required to eradicate original sin and achieve salvation, and if God wishes all to be saved, then unbaptized infants would have to be condemned to hell. The frank unfairness of this caused Saint Augustine to allow that they might exist on the fringe (*limbus*) of hell, known as Limbo. Saint Augustine is trapped. He edges away until my father says sorry to bring up a superstition, but walking backward is bad luck.

Saint Augustine retreats, exhausted, into a corner.

Immediately joining us are choruses of Catholic schoolchildren: But, Sister! If I'm walking to school with my Buddhist friend and she's hit by a car, and I pour water on her head, does it count? Why should the babies from India have to crawl around in Limbo?

I have to leave my historical painting as incomplete; I do not yet know enough to include someone who can answer those children, gleeful that they've caught theologians in a puzzle.

I do not agree that life is "one shot" and only art affords the luxury of endless rewrites. Every life is also riddled with additions, overlays, new knowledge, and revisions that change ideas and recollections. Discoveries—even after someone's death— drift back and attach to memories, refiguring them: I found out that Vó was not my blood grandmother. My father waited a substantial interval after she died (to insure that we would never accord her less than full respect?) before showing us a picture of a young woman, Francesca Borges. After giving birth to him, she succumbed to *"a morte roxa,"* or purple death (as in "purpura fever"), the Portuguese term for dying in childbirth.

Out of Vó's death—long after the fact—rose up this mirror image of my own face. I stared at the photograph. Now I could clarify scenes in my past, when busybodies pinched my face and, using the nickname for Francesca, said, "Ai, you look like Xica." In her wedding portrait, Xica holds a bouquet with white ribbons looped to form auxiliary flowers. It cost my grandfather a week's salary in the Azores; its abundance tells me that she inspired people to love with abandon.

I do look like her, with her large eyes, one slightly turned inward, though I continue farther into age. By not surviving past twenty-six, Xica is set as a perfect youthful cameo, like Lee, and so this grandmother I never knew existed, this earlier version of me, dwells in counterpart with the beauty and short life of my friend.

Clementina embellished these revelations: Vó worried as a stepmother about measuring up, about being judged an American above reproach, about replacing a ghost. At one point, the pressures drove her to episodes of weeping and hitting her head against a wall. She snapped as much as I did back in my own dead phase.

No wonder tidiness had been a passion. A joked-about quirk of character stretched back to the fear of not doing right, some quandary about fitting in, not so different from my own childhood silences. That incident with the dead canary—naturally she would ache over the loss of the wild singer she kept inside, like

The Baptism, Julius Stewart, United States, 1855–1919

that brilliant part of herself, the party girl and storyteller, chattering and messy but finally caged until it died. I doubt she would have ever confessed her collapse to me, but had she known in greater detail about mine, she might have claimed me in her heart as heir to the same secrets.

Lee, dying, wordlessly drew her parents to her side. Vó, though she pushed almost everyone away from her own deathbed, chose in her own manner to speak across silence to me. I do not recall ever going to a museum with Vó, but one day she helped me step inside a painting.

This is what happened. I usually glanced with the quick register that many of us reserve for so-called society paintings at *The Baptism* (1892) by the American artist Julius Stewart (1855–1919), in the Los Angeles County Museum of Art. Certainly its size (almost 80 inches by 120) is enough to arrest, for a beat or two, the high-clicking inner metronome that keeps us speeding from room to room. We pass on, ticking off what we see. But I never lost the suspicion that a mystery was shimmering out from *The Baptism*, a sound wave calling out to passersby. One afternoon, recalling Lee's pleasure in going slowly through museums, I stopped and sat down with the painting.

On the face of it, the composition is lush but staid, painstaking in its naturalistic details—the shadows in a silk cascade, the lace cutwork accurate to the width of an eyelash. Family and friends, emissaries from a cosseted existence, are gathered for the christening playing itself out in the background. A young mother on a divan, enervated from childbirth, consumes the foreground.

On this particular visit, I noticed the purple flower in the mother's right hand, held on her lap. Purple death! How had I missed what had always been right in front of me? The young woman is telling us that she's dying! Focal point and center, she is insisting to anyone who will bother to pause and watch with her that what takes up most of *The Baptism* is death. And suddenly the whole sprawl of life, these characters and their varying depths of sorrow, wariness, or devotion, and the bloom of everything observable or ultimately unknowable, burst open on the canvas as if I knew these people. I do know them; we all do.

Vó and Xica gave me that Rosetta-stone of a detail, the key hiding in a color. Even without my grandmothers' history guiding me into this canvas, how could I have missed the anguish that has sealed the eyes of the husband and caused the dying woman's father to kneel, devastated, behind her? A sister wears a purple sash in counterpoint to the flower of death and inclines her head toward her beloved sibling, as if assuming the same languid posture so that God might take her, too. Why had I ever judged this scene stiff and refined?

I heard some pens scratching, and noticed two college girls with notebooks. When I asked what they were doing, they groaned and said they were stuck having to write up for their UCLA art history class what they saw "in this, like, totally stupid old painting." It's how promptly fortune scooted them over that impresses me as hilarious, the kind of surprise that can sear off the fat parts of a day and leave a story behind.

I mentioned the purple flower and my guesses, and then the schoolteacher in me interrupted their fierce note-taking. "And what do *you* think?" I asked.

"Oh," said one of them, grinning, "we think you're doing just fine."

They joined me on the viewing bench. If swimming for me is like moving in a painting, then this was like having others join me to swim around in a painting. One of them pointed out that Stewart loses his articulated line with a bizarre corridor reflected in the mirror over the fireplace. The rough brush strokes suggest infinity. Was that crone with her nose in a prayer book the mother, jealous of the pretty daughter gaining attention in death? "Creepy!" said the student, overjoyed.

They took over instructing me. That tree trunk on the tapestry crowns the godmother's hair with an eerie gremlin! What will become of the boy in the sailor's suit, averting his face from everyone? As a grown-up, will he be incapable of disavowing the stance of the bereft child? Look at the fright on the minister's face! The clouds trace celestial writing onto the windows. The curtain is a gateway to paradise.

The UCLA students and I had a farewell coffee in the museum's courtyard, a communion to add to our sharing of Baptism. Sacramental rites wait to be replicated in our quotidian lives: simple grace. Unlofty eucharists. We listen to people in a painting howl with grief. I order coffee, and strangers transport me back two decades and recall for me my lost friend; the days when Lee and I visited here, two college allies, had been waiting to be made new.

Having led me to the interior of the painting, Xica and Vó invited me to peer farther with them into the realm of the dead, contained in this artistic rendering of Baptism, to consolidate what I felt about Lee.

By putting birth, death, and redemption on view at the same time, *The Baptism* cuts clear to the essence of her. In that simple act of walking me to her parents' door before her surgery, for instance, she was mindful that death was present, but so was the grace of conquering it through mundane gestures. This impulse is not far removed from the astonishing, truest precept of Baptism: *Life, death, burial, resurrection, and grace are enacted all at once.* This sacrament condenses the tenets of the Christian faith—Christ was born, crucified, buried, and rose again in the flesh. We are asked to die in water and come out living. Saint Paul declared that water is a tomb, and also a womb from which we are resurrected in spirit and body; in a flow of water, we die and find ourselves simultaneously, newly alive, "grafted into the paschal mystery," as the Second Vatican Council frames it.

That is the impossible, expansive message of Baptism. Everything, all at once, attendant upon grace. Instead of viewing existence as a series of moments lined up like beads on a string, to be flung away in terror when we reach the last one, we are asked to see a constant mesh of life and death, the visible and invisible. We are enjoined to rejoice with more fervor by not being afraid of detecting that death is barnacled to every single day from birth. Baptism proclaims this in brazen fullness. Death bides its time, but—as painter Julius Stewart confirms, as my friend showed me—it is never out of the room.

In her journal, Lee recorded terror, but she also visited the Oatlands Mansion with its huge maze, picked sod worms off the broccoli in her garden, admired a postcard of a giant trout from Tucumcari, ate ice cream, and was amused about landing in a hospital room near Reagan's after he had been shot: "something to tell my grandchildren." These episodes of normality—preserved insofar as she wrote them down—are infused with poignant radiance because death was so near.

When is it not, for any of us, at any time? When is Baptism's convulsive all-at-once narration not our perplexing destiny? Lee's photo, when she knows she is ill, glows with life and death at once; so did that first Baptism in the River Jordan.

The tableau I began at Daniel's Baptism was missing the most crucial figures. I should have painted Christ stepping into the river, bridging the physical and spiritual, the new and the traditional. He did not disdain participation in a ceremony that had its roots in the ritual washings and purifications of Judaism. (*Baptism* comes from the Greek for "cleansing.") These rites, along with circumcision, were exterior signs of one's faith.

Various sects were veering toward an emphasis on righteousness and the coming of the holy kingdom, on interior repentance rather than outward sign. When Saint John the Baptist, one of the exhorters, ministered to Jesus in the Jordan, the Spirit descended as Jesus accepted his destiny of crucifixion according to the Father's will. An invocation to the Trinity therefore became part of the Christian rite. Christ's human blood was to be the connecting river between death and redemption. Earth blended with heaven, and the fate of death was made inseparable from the promise of rebirth: An acceptance of all realities, time frames, and mysteries bloomed in one powerful instant.

Nature and spirit were welded together, mingled in water. Human beings and their hopeful symbols—this is what divinity seeks to make incarnate. An ascension of actual bodies, the living and the dead, was promised at that first Baptism, and what a compelling promise; what a consolation. Heaven would not disdain the corporeal.

Onto my grand painting of historical figures, I want to add Saint Paul, who declared Baptism as a celebration of reality—fire, speech, water, air, oil, earth.

Saint Thomas Aquinas should have been included because of his suggestion that just as an infant is fully human but dependent upon its mother, a baby receiving the spiritual rebirth of Baptism could be a full-fledged member in Mother Church. That calms me about the notion of baptizing infants. As for those babies crawling around in Limbo: The current catechism affirms that original sin exists, but that it lacks the character of a personal fault. Many current theologians point out that original sin was never meant to be the sacrament's sole focus. An all-at-once evocation of mysteries is more vitally attuned to that first Baptism.

Just as "baptism of blood" would save a martyr, and "baptism of desire" could be enough for a person of faith who died before receiving the sacrament, so too God must have a way of absorbing into holiness an innocent person who dies before a ceremony of initiation. The mysteries of original sin would be subordinate to the mysteries of grace and justice.

This all-at-once baptismal manifesto is about hope, but its narrative is firmly at odds with the way we tell stories. It refuses to line up causes and effects in digestible story form. Actions that rise and complicate and wind to some semblance of a finish are what engage us. We cannot be comfortable with a plunge into life, death, burial, and resurrection all at once, an ultra-collapsed story line, formless as water, a terrible, plotless grandness.

Yet our own mortality makes precisely such a demand upon us. When Macabéa, the hapless typist of Clarice Lispector's novel *The Hour of the Star*, lies dying after a car hits her in Rio de Janeiro, her dreams about being Marilyn Monroe explode alive: Every person's death makes him or her a star of reality and infinity. We do not disappear; we become "vigorous air." At her starry hour, as blood pours from Macabéa's wounds, the narrator reflects: "I shall go on until I reach that point where the atmosphere finishes. . . . Does my breath deliver me to God?"

The nobility asked of us is breathtaking because we sign up for a battle that we know we cannot win. Yet we remain admirably cognizant enough of death to seek its defeat through efforts, however small, to rewrite the world closer to our discoveries within it. My husband, Michael, went to a docent's talk on *The Baptism*, and when nothing was said about death, he pointed out the purple flower. The curator later sent us a note thanking us, saying that he was prompted to recall that purple flowers figured with a similar symbolism in Victorian art.

A year ago, Michael returned to the museum and reported that the sign now mentions words to the effect that the woman in the foreground seems gravely ill. Whether someone came to this on his or her own, or several people did, or I might have contributed, I have added my intent, if not my actual voice, to a change somewhere, real words across a silence to attach themselves to an artwork that will speak to others.

There are many such ways to redesign the physical plane, but how to resurrect bodily someone who is gone?

It is the person we long for, not the elegant lesson. Memory, for all its misfirings, should be humbler than it is, and nostalgia cannot be trusted to honor the dead. It extrapolates from the known, makes us construct who someone would be, based solely on what he or she was. If we resort only to the inaccuracies of memory, then everyone we love is at one point finished and attests to our failure of imagination. (I am not referring to revisionism, which whitewashes the past, but to the effort to send our imaginations in pursuit of what Apollinaire called "the truth behind the true.") I want people to possess stories they did not have the chance to enact while alive. I still want my loved ones to surprise me.

Vó never went to Portugal with me, but I can imagine her at my side on the balcony of my friend Hélia Correia's house in Lisbon, looking at the ossuary boxes in Benfica Cemetery. Hélia explains that after five years, bodies have disintegrated down to their bones and may be moved from the earth into these boxes to make room for a new generation of the dead. Hope is said to reside in marrow, and we might picture skeletons dancing in the air, bodies ascending.

Vó accompanies me on my pilgrimage on her behalf. A Plexiglas box housing a statue marks the site where Mary first appeared in a tree—long since ripped up, branches, trunk, and roots, by the seekers of relics. The flood of humanity crowding into Fátima, all that unfathomable desire and solitude, represents the baptismal ocean of the twenty-first century. How do we find blessings in this sea, much less anyone discernible? What words can approach such enormity?

Vó and I push through the hordes of needy, wailing people to put her picture with those of hundreds of other petitioners. I lose Vó, who is in her element, a party girl again, wandering off to chat in her native language. Others nearby hurl wax figures into an incinerator to ask God for mercy—a wax heart to cure anguish; a wax lung for a father with emphysema; legs, breasts, livestock, whatever is ailing. I see a couple sobbing as they throw a wax baby into the flames, and I cannot breathe. There is no such thing as a permanent miracle when we beg to be spared.

I stumble away but encounter a gypsy girl chanting, "Lady, lady, I'm dying of hunger." And I am arrested in silence, not sure what to do.

Vó grabs me and says, furiously, that I should have been holding her hand, that she does not want to lose me. She drags the gypsy girl over to the ladies' room and scrubs her at the sink while complaining about how filthy the washroom is—such human disgrace, so close to a sacred venue!

Lee always wanted to visit Portugal with me. She might paint me adhering my grandmother's face to the site of a miracle, hope and hopelessness arrested together, all-at-once death and life, and later the rebirth of her having painted such a moment.

Or it would be a hot day, and Lee would suggest that we find a drink. She and Vó and the gypsy girl and I would walk past the burning hearts and booths with their bins of wax body parts and stop for a bottle of Luso water at a table smeared with Sumol pineapple soda. Vó would laugh and say, I guess I have to clean up this entire country, and she would hunt down a towel to wipe the table. The gypsy girl might run away after we fed her. Or she would tell us a story that would change our lives. Or nothing too piercing would happen. We would be family, friends, and strangers keeping company, water and words, the ordinary miracle of saying *this, now, with you,* this suffices me. Even if we dream them up, these are the moments that baptize the planet, carve through sky, shape the trees. My Vó's face is melted upon other yearning faces in a location of miracles. Because Lee was radiant while dying in Washington in autumn, that place also retains more vigorous air. Countless people have breathed in those defeats of death and will exhale them for someone else to take in. As light as inspiration, we enter the bodies of others for as long as the world abides.

SOURCES

Thomas Bokenkotter, *A Concise History of the Catholic Church, Revised Edition* (New York: Doubleday, 1966).

Philip Larkin, "Water," from *The Whitsun Weddings* (New York: Random House, 1964).

C. S. Lewis, *The Joyful Christian: 127 Readings* (New York: Macmillan, 1977).

Richard P. McBrien, *Catholicism* (Minneapolis: Winston, 1981).

John F. McDonald, *The Sacraments in the Christian Life* (Middlegreen, England: St. Paul, 1983).

Karl Rahner, *Hominisation* (London: Burns & Oates, 1965).

Liam G. Walsh, O.P., *The Sacraments of Initiation* (London: Geoffrey Chapman Theology Library, 1988).

PENANCE

PATRICIA HAMPL

Bill Jack, my old friend from grade school, has reminded me. It all remains indelible and permanently mysterious to him too: those St. Paul Saturday nights in spring, lilac time, the years before Daylight Savings, when it was already dark by seven o'clock. Monsignor Cullinan, little barrel of a body, shuffling up the slight incline of Lexington in an oddly staccato way. And Father Slattery—remember Slattery? Handsome and remote. He always accompanied Monsignor, and slowed down his long-legged gait to match the old man's. A priestly Mutt and Jeff. They were returning from their after-dinner stroll, headed back to St. Luke's to hear Saturday night confessions. In the cobalt light, their cassocks slapped softly against their trouser legs.

Easy to bring them back. They come up Lex from Grand, a busy street even then. Pause at Summit, their destination the pale gray hulk of St. Luke's on the far corner. From the deep pocket of his cassock, each priest roots out a big handkerchief. Then, waving these white squares above their black shapes, they step off the sidewalk. Cars screech to a halt. They proceed across the avenue, holding up traffic, their white flags fluttering in the growing gloom of early evening. They disappear through the church side-door to the basement church where the Catholics are already patiently lined up, waiting to present their sins.

That's how it was, late 1950s, even well into the 1960s, past Vatican II, which ended in 1965. On a Saturday night, this typical exchange: someone, probably my brother, calling out, "Wanna go to the movie at the Uptown?" And one of us replies, "Sure. Go to confession first? Movie doesn't start till 7:30." The easy presence of sacramental life all around us. *Wanna go to the Uptown, confession first? Sure, fine. Malts after? Bridgemans'll still be open. OK, sure.*

The casual assumption of religion, the unapologetic publicness of it on the streets of our neighborhood, the parish priests (in those years there were several for a big parish like St. Luke's) walking along Summit in the late afternoon, reading their breviaries. You were supposed to move out of their way if, absorbed in prayer, they happened to stray to your side of the pavement as you passed by, though it was considered a nice touch if a priest raised his head briefly from the prayerbook and smiled (Father Kennedy, the cute one, sometimes winked). Nobody spoke— oh no. They had to read their Office, it was a dark sin not to— their kind of sin, not a sin we needed to bother with, but a sin nonetheless. Leave them to it.

Signs of grace abounded. Nuns dipped into the side door of St. Luke's, "for a little adoration," as they airily said. Children were excused from class and trooped over to the church from the grade school next door to sing, in birdy voices, the dank sentiments of the "Dies irae" at weekday funerals when the professional quavering contralto of Alma Quince (no kidding) was elsewhere engaged. It was not uncommon to see people, women especially, walking along one of the parish side streets, Oxford or Milton, saying the rosary, hands in pockets, fingers passing over the beads, lips faintly moving. Sometimes the rosary was held, two-fisted, right in front. A bit showy maybe, and only for older ladies understood to be widowed or otherwise alone in the world. But in such cases, this public piety was the badge of a solitude well employed.

We were surrounded by worship, buoyed up by gestures of belief, as if many wings were flapping all about us, like the white hankies miraculously stopping traffic on Summit, keeping us suspended in the peculiar vacancy of our ordinary lives, which in this way were not allowed to pass for ordinary at all. *The Kingdom of God is within you, boys and girls. Never forget that.*

How ever could we?

Yet, standing in the long line trailing from the confessional with the white card marked FATHER KENNEDY (Never go to Monsignor! we warned each other—he'll give you five rosaries, all fifteen Mysteries), it was hard not to feel hopeless. In Frank O'Connor's autobiographical short story, "First Confession," the sensitive child Jackie suffers a soul-shivering terror at the thought of entering the little box for the first time: He must confess his intention to kill, presumably with the breadknife she herself wields, his grandmother, a fierce and filthy peasant who has just come to live with the family. "She's a horrible woman, Father," he says, explaining his motive. "She takes porter. And she ates the potatoes off the table with her hands. . . . And she gives pinnies to Nora and she doesn't give no pinnies to me because she knows I can't stand her." She is an aesthetic outrage. She goes barefoot and is a harridan, and his father—worst betrayal—takes her part against Jackie. "Me heart is broken," he finally says, "and wan night in bed I made it up the way I'd kill her."

Jackie bears the burden of a sin which is immense, overwhelming, perhaps unforgivable, certainly criminal. This sort of childhood confession trauma, it is often suggested, is the source of the notorious "Catholic guilt" adults with pre–Vatican II childhoods are alleged to lug around the rest of their (our) lives to the arch amusement and dismay of the less churched.

But my problem was just the opposite. I had been instructed, along with everyone in Sister Julia's second grade class, to make a careful examination of conscience before entering the confessional to recite my sins. This entailed ticking one's way down the Ten Commandments, flushing out faults in a bookkeeperly fashion, accumulating a decent tally to present in the confessional. ("If you can't remember *exactly* how many times you disobeyed your mother, Sheila, then you may offer an estimate." – "By the day or by the week, Sister?" – "Either way, dear, either way.")

But what, exactly, could I come up with in the way of presentable sins? My life—all the world around me—I saw glumly, bred a terrible absence of activity of any kind useful to the purpose. Forget mortal sins—they were in a class far above anything we could hope to muster. (*"You are unlikely to encounter any mortal sins, boys and girls, as you make your Examination of Conscience, but remember, a venial sin must still be understood as a sin of consequence."*) The scant sweepings of venial sins I was left to scavenge were hardly inspiring.

If the Kingdom of God was within me, as Sister claimed, well and good. And I could feel it—wasn't that what happiness was? But where was Satan? Where his works and pomps? Didn't they—sins and sinning—constitute the other part of life, hidden but vast, a kind of thrilling hot breath seething somewhere beyond the everyday life whose vapid ether pervaded St. Luke's and which we took in measured sips? The mistral of evil, the whirlwind of wrongdoing—wasn't that what we were talking about here?

It wasn't that I felt myself to be in a state of perpetual grace, already perfected, enclosed within a spiritual sanctuary bounded away from the reality of sin and its complications. None of that. I was simply disappointed by the quality of sin available to me, the predictability and flat anti-narrative tedium of my lists. Even the tallies seemed foolish and mingy. *Bless me, Father, it's been two weeks since my last confession. I disobeyed my folks, um, ten times . . . maybe more, maybe twenty times. . . . No, ten is about right. . . .*

It was hopeless. I went through a childhood of Saturday night recitations feeling guilty, not for my sins, but for the boredom of my life. There was no *story* in any of this confessing. My life was a grocery list—or worse, it was an antique clerk's desk into whose pigeonholes I divvied up my sins like shopkeepers' bills come due: so many lies, so many disobediences. The Fourth Commandment, for years, was my old standby. What else was there? Not much. "Unkindness?" Think of crossing the street so I didn't have to walk to school with creepy Vivian Mert who could really use a pal. That counts. "Unrighteous Anger"? My brother Peter's taunting face rose before me: Oh yes, anger—but he started it!

One Saturday night, my mother gently drew me aside (like most families in the parish, we went to confession together, each of us waiting our turn—Mother and Dad, with breathtaking nonchalance, entering Monsignor's box because his line was shortest). "Darling," she said softly as we knelt together in the pew, saying the Hail Marys we had been given as penance, "you have to lower your voice in the confessional. We could hear everything you said." The shame of it! But the deeper shame was that I had exposed the paltry stuff I was handing over—that she could hear me ticking off my mild infractions, that Peter was now in smug possession of my admission of a sin on his account, though, as he well knew, *he started it*. I wished, with a passionate disregard for the state of my soul, that I hadn't confessed that one at all. It shouldn't count as a sin; it was a clear case of self-defense. I had only included it so that I had something to dish out besides my usual lug of disobediences.

This public humiliation was the same as the private one I'd long carried within me: Nothing much to report from this quarter of the sinning population, Father. Just as a disappointed wife gazes blankly before her, thinking there must be more happiness to life than her dull round, at ten I stared out disconsolately thinking there must be more sin somewhere, somewhere. Curiously, I developed the sensation that I must be lying, that I would naturally be suspected of not reporting the real stuff when I kept showing up, week after week, year after year, with these predictable, featureless sins. Sister had been clear: Making a "bad confession" was worse than any sin you were covering up to begin with. This, indeed, *would* be a mortal sin, even if you were only holding back venial sins. But as far as I could tell, I was giving all I had to give—and more. The problem was that, spiritually speaking, my soul was the flyover.

In a way, puberty saved me. Finally, I approached the confessional in a cold sweat. Finally, the hot breath of stealth and secrecy breathed upon me. This was what all the shouting was about. More than the sudden alarm of sex, it was this: I experienced the self at stake.

I hesitated in the dark basement church, shilly-shallying between Slattery and Kennedy—which one to present with what, after all, was my real first confession? Monsignor, of course, was unthinkable. I'd always been a Kennedy penitent, an instinct for his lightness, the cheerful wink along the sidewalk. But this was something else again, something that, I intuited, required a more stately impersonality. I pulled aside the mud-colored drape of Slattery's confessional, and knelt in the sudden dark, waiting for his hand to slide open the little window veiled with tallow-colored muslin where, at last and with the desperate "contrite heart" we had been told was the proper state for the penitent, I would confess to "thoughts," and yes, to "deeds" as well.

I had decided to lead with my usual tally of disobediences and "unkind thoughts" and so forth, plenty of those at the ready. They would serve as a sort of hors d'oeuvre, a warm-up for this new thing of the night, the alarming, hungry shadows of desire. Then the plunge, gratefully grabbing the exquisite euphemism provided by the "Examination of Conscience" under the Sixth Commandment at the back of the *Baltimore Catechism*—"impure thoughts and deeds, Father...."

"Alone or with others?" Slattery murmured smoothly.

With *others*? What was he *thinking* of? "Alone, Father!" I cried, the shock hurling my voice aloud, out of the confessional whisper.

He lowered his own voice slightly, and in the same uninsinuating, unconcerned tone, suggested I might listen to music on the hi-fi at such times.

"We don't have a hi-fi, Father."

Well, did we have a radio? Yes, we had a radio. So listen to the radio. Or TV was good.

Then, a couple of Our Fathers and a handful of Hail Marys, and I was in the light again.

The dark cubby of the confessional, the low whisper of the private voice rendering to God not what is God's but what is the Devil's—it was an astonishing procedure. It offered, in return for the humble acknowledgement of the broken truths of the self, nothing short of a new life. Here was the baptismal promise beating along the pulse—not an idea but an intense throb of liberation. There is no way to describe (to over-describe) the transport of being shriven.

The great Teresa, whose ecstasy Bernini somehow managed to capture in the unlikely medium of stone, appears knocked unconscious in her orgasmic union with the Divine. That, presumably, is the Eucharist, feeding on the Body of God, losing oneself in that penetrating love. It is meant to be the greatest religious sensation imaginable. That's why it looks like sex: ecstasy must. It is the transcendence of self, the subsuming of the intense nothing of the individual into the All.

Confession, on the other hand, at least as we experienced it at St. Luke's, provided an ecstasy of self, the full return to one's own life, but cleansed, ready to be lived anew. The unbelievable second chance, nothing short of rebirth. Absolution returned the soul to itself, back into the housing of the body and its mind—but new, fresh, ready to roll.

Confession was not an experience of self-inflation or egotism, nor (once the initial shock of declaration was absorbed) was it an exercise in humiliation. It was, rather, a moment of personal liberation: to emerge from the time-out-of-time darkness of the little box, overwhelmed with gratitude, and in possession of a wondrous discovery—that we are creatures born for radiance. Our natural state is to be light, free, ready for the next thing.

Maybe this liberating sensation was just a surfeit of relief, bred of a ruinous scrupulosity. It is tempting to dismiss it that way. But the old-style confession, the kind that still fires the popular imagination and has fascinated and marked writers in the supposedly nonreligious (even anti-religious) passing century—Joyce, Mary McCarthy come to mind—this was, finally, a sacramental act. If by "sacramental" we mean an authentic, if mysterious, change wrought within the human heart by ritual gestures and words, murmurs and the absolving movement of an anonymous hand poised above a bowed head.

It is strange that the sacrament of Penance should be so thoroughly associated with privacy, even secrecy. Frame again the classic tableau: In the hush of the confessional, penitent and confessor huddle in the dark, a scrim veiling their faces, as if the exchange between them were so intensely intimate that it partakes of the sacred, and therefore, like the face of God, cannot be looked upon directly. Holy, holy, holy—the paradox at the heart of sin. And—as the confessional moment suggests even more absolutely—private, private, private.

It was not always so. In fact, the invention of the sacrament, the felt need for it, was rooted in the ancient world's elemental commitment to the community, not in modernity's abstract concern for the individual. The sacrament was conceived as a public reconciliation, necessary to the very existence of the congregation. For if, after the drenching purification of Baptism, people did still persist in sin (a fact hard to get around even in the ecstatic and apocalyptic early church, as Paul's letters attest again and again), then there had to be a method, a mechanism even, for reconversion. The church needed a vehicle for the safe return of souls (and their bodies) to the congregation. But it was a severe sacrament. Like Baptism, Penance was understood in its early form as a one-time-only event. Without this second-chance clause, Baptism itself was in jeopardy, and all the other sacaramental integuments binding Christians together risked disintegration. Penance was group life insurance for the church, not an individual policy.

Still, even in this early conception of the sacrament, the individual counts—and counts absolutely. *Which one of you with a hundred sheep, if he lost one, would fail to leave the ninety-nine in the desert and go after the missing one till he found it? And when he found it, would he not joyfully take it on his shoulders, and then, when he got home, call together his friends and neighbors, saying to them, "Rejoice with me, I have found my sheep that was lost." In the same way, I tell you, there will be more rejoicing in heaven over one sinner repenting than over ninety-nine people who have no need of repentance.*

At this scriptural moment (Luke 15:4–7), which might be marked as the inaugural instant of the sacrament of Penance, the individual, thanks to the efficiency of metaphor, is understood to be fundamentally, not extraneously, a member of a larger integrity. A sheep in a treasured herd. That is precisely where the individual's value—which is great—lies. The joy in finding the repentant sinner is not the kind of satisfaction to be found in the therapist's office, where the lost and scattered shards of a life are excavated and carefully pieced together to form that essential thing: a life worth living bred of a life story worth telling. Penance was intended to heal a different wound—not the break between a person and individual consciousness (or a personal past), but that between the self and the community, which, for the ancient, was the core of existence.

"The community" itself was terribly fragile, of course. The little bands of Christian cultists, held together initially by exhorting letters and apocalyptic fervor (and by the inwardness that oppression breeds), were hardly in a position to lose a single sheep.

In fact, one of the first ecclesiastic acts of the early Christian communities was to ensure a method of re-admission to the fold for those who had strayed.

Public shunning was sometimes employed by an early Christian group as a way of handling sin, and this severity did serve to reaffirm the orthodoxy of the faith. But it was not the answer to the more essential question—how to keep the community viable. Shunning and expulsion could not be a permanent solution for the ancient church. The canny apostolic wisdom of the early church apparently understood that even as it was engaged in the business of legitimizing itself by hammering out its dogma, it had to find wiggle room, a side door through which the sinner could return home. By the second century, the Shepherd of Hermas, for example, was allowing a "second chance" to penitent sinners. A clear recognition that Baptism alone did not suffice in the battle against sin. Too much leniency jeopardized the great divide Baptism was meant to create between the unconverted and the Christian. But no leniency at all might mean no church.

"Confession"—a precise recitation of sins large and small—didn't figure into the sacrament. There was nothing, really, to confess because the ancient community already knew the penitent's sins: They were common knowledge to the congregation, not a personal flaw held in the secrecy of the heart. That was the whole point. This was public business, with an essentially public sacrament fashioned to handle it. Ordinary personal imperfections were not seen as the business of the sacrament—such spiritual work belonged to the life of prayer, to supplication, fasting, and almsgiving—the usual round of Christian behavior. Penance, being by its very nature a public sacrament that addressed infractions of the social order, simply wasn't necessary for these inevitable human failings. Early Christianity was a radical religion, a break with the old gods, and it was a purifying, often ascetic cult. But it was not nosy, not small-minded and neurotic. Its concerns were the expansive ones of its immense apocalyptic vision and its urge to survive. Penance couldn't afford to be petty. The sacrament existed to mend those places where the individual threatened the congregation.

The only instance in the ancient church of what we think of as private penance was the reconciliation of the dying. For ancients the deathbed was the vestibule to eternal life. It was not uncommon, for instance, for a pagan—Saint Augustine's father, Patricius, was one—to hold off Baptism until just before death. This was a kind of have-your-cake-and-eat-it-too strategy for a pagan teetering between two worlds: The demands of the Christian life need only be upheld briefly so that, confident of the soul's purity, the newly baptized could enter paradise after having enjoyed a pretty fine time on earth, unencumbered by the strictures of Christian practice.

By the late second century and into the early third century, most urban centers had developed the concept of Penance even further. They created "orders of penitents" roughly parallel to the catechumens, the pre-baptismal converts-in-training who could "hear the Word" but did not yet consume the Body and Blood, or participate in the other sacramental and liturgical acts of the church. The Christian community encouraged and supported returning sinners during their period in the penitential order—quite the opposite of shunning.

There was even a public liturgy (praising God's mercy for their return) which restored penitents to the status of faithful Christians. The early church was *grateful* to have them back. Far from wishing to shame them with their sins, the intense, vulnerable early communities rejoiced in the return of the stray sheep. These early congregations lived close to the Prodigal Son story—another public penitent whose sins, so obvious to the social order of the ancient civic mind, hardly needed to be "confessed."

Key to all of this civic forgiveness were repentance and reformation—understood as nothing less than full reconversion, not just the I'm-sorry-give-me-my-ten-Hail-Marys of so many pre–Vatican II memories. This is where the image of sackcloth and ashes comes from, which the modern mind finds either histrionic or unnecessarily humiliating. The community had to see, in public weeping, prayer, fasting, and almsgiving, clear symbols of repentance so that the reclamation of the individual into the congregation could be entire. If the ancient sinner were, like an anxious modern, simply slipping into the therapist's office to choke out a painful tale, then coming out the side door in sackcloth and ashes and all the rest of the theatrical signaling of repentance would indeed be a strange, even sadistic exercise. But the individual who acquiesced to the penance of the early church was being reunited with the community, not with himself. Penance was not a psychological but a sociological act.

By the sixth century, few people entered the order of penitents voluntarily. The process had calcified into a canonical procedure whose legalisms undermined the impulse among most Christians to pursue reconciliation. Penance degenerated into a coercive penalty rather than a voluntary method for rehabilitation. The heart had gone out of the thing. Those who did voluntarily join the order of penitents, the *conversi*, typically did so in the spirit of those who, today, enter vowed religious orders. It became their lives, not a part of life.

The public nature of Penance, coupled with various struggles with heretical groups, finally caused the sacrament to become more rigorous—and more punitive. Perhaps the most troubling long-term effect of this legalistic direction was that, like Baptism, the sacrament of Penance was allowed only once in a lifetime as the early church developed its thinking on the subject. There was a contradiction here, of course, with basic gospel teaching of ongoing, even constant, forgiveness.

But there it was—and there it stayed until the medieval church, thanks to the evangelizing Irish monks, reversed the process and drew the newly converted Celts not only to Baptism but to the exuberant confession of their sins. Which brought the sacrament, inevitably, to the brink of storytelling and the magic healing art of narrative, as if to the doorstep of its true destiny.

There was an interesting exception to the dispiriting legalization of the sacrament in the Roman church. In fifth-century Rome many Christians not under the strictures of canonical penance became ceremonial penitents during Lent—the period in the church year that had always been (and remains to this day) the time of final preparation for Baptism and entrance into the Church. As the order of penitents declined, these Lenten ceremonial penitents increased. By the tenth century the practice was so thoroughly absorbed into the Church that all Christians were expected to observe a period of Lenten penance. The Fourth Lateran Council of 1215 finally made it legal: It demanded annual confession of all baptized Catholics.

The evangelizing of the Celtic monks, who appear to have borrowed some of their methods from the Eastern church (which was usually less legalistic than Rome), introduced the practice of confessing one's sins in a way that begins to look familiar to us.

The order of penitents of the early church had been a onetime chance to pull up your socks, a repetition of the catechumenate for those who presumably had not been properly inducted to begin with. Private confession of the sort the Celtic monks were introducing was, on the other hand, a repeatable procedure. Since it wasn't initially a canonical practice (that is, it did not include a public act of rehabilitation overseen by the bishop), the sacrament became more intimate. What was required was a (private) recitation of offenses (the centrality of this act is what led to the procedure being called "confession" sometime around the eighth or ninth centuries) and—very important—a penitential act of some kind to make "satisfaction." Different sins had different satisfactions and these were listed in books called "penitentials" and were duly assigned to the confessing penitent.

Although all of this sounds rather canonical itself, the big difference was that the monks (who were not necessarily priests— another distinction that endures within monasticism into our own times) offered a method for unloading the burden of sin that involved no social stigma, no public exposure. And in place of the one chance on earth to wipe the slate clean before the Final Judgment, they offered a repeatable pattern of forgiveness in the natural round of life.

There were political and sociological reasons for the shift in emphasis from a public to more private understanding of penance. But perhaps the radical change Christianity had to absorb concerning the nature of conversion and the Second Coming lies at the theological heart of the movement from public to private reconciliation.

After all, the primitive church didn't expect to be on the planet very long. The whole point of conversion was expressed in the liturgies of Advent, which are the earliest of all the church liturgies and express more explicitly than the Easter mysteries the apocalyptic core assumptions of the first Christians. Their fundamental belief concerned the end time, the coming of the Kingdom. And, they believed, coming *soon*.

As the Church moved out of this epiphanic and apocalyptic period, and steadied into the long haul of figuring out what Christian *life* (not merely *conversion*) would mean, it is natural that the liturgies and sacraments meant to sustain this new life would also undergo alteration and interpretation. And if Baptism was the great cult act dividing the Christian from a personal (pagan) past, it was also the moment that separated the early Christian from a (pagan) world, putting him at odds with the political and civic order of the time. But when, early in the fourth century,

Christianity ended its renegade status and became the state religion of the Roman Empire, Baptism itself, while still forever decisive, came away just slightly nicked.

Perhaps it became impossible for the moment of Baptism to bear the alarming edge of radical conversion of the primitive church when conversion was no longer purely a wild overturning of one's world but a solemn admission into a prevailing civic system. Baptism began to be more a form of solemn joining up, not the dislocating, dangerous act of sedition of previous ages.

Religion shares with art the habit of paradox. That is what lies at the core of their formal power—the ability to hold contradictions in balance. The success of Christianity was its domestication into the dailiness of civic life, but this empowerment was also paradoxically the source of its great loss—the high pitch of the apocalyptic message. The held breath went out of Christianity. Christ was not coming tomorrow, not even the day after tomorrow. What was waited for now began to be understood in more personal—and more metaphoric—terms. Now, in the new safety of a civic religion, the individual Christian had occasion to ponder sin, sin large and small but sin constant and filled always with the idiosyncrasy of a particular life. The Christian community was less exactly the vulnerable herd, jealous of its individual sheep.

The community was morphing into the state. It was not above using the authority and brute power of the state to subdue heretical groups threatening its hegemony and orthodoxy. By 405 (less than a century since the adoption of Christianity as the imperial religion) Augustine, bishop of Hippo Regius in North

Africa, had "accepted that the Roman state could bring to bear the force of its own laws so as to 'reunite' Donatist congregations to the Catholic church under threat of punishment," according to Peter Brown, his biographer. That fussy euphemism—*reunite*—has the same bad smell we recognize from the Soviet "normalization" of Czechoslovakia after 1968 or American "pacification" of Vietnamese villages. And as Brown—and history itself—make clear, Augustine's decision had profound consequences. In upholding "the view that the structures of authority that gave cohesion to profane society might be called upon to support the Catholic church," Augustine, paradoxically, attacked the intimate structures of Christian community even as he succeeded in his obsession, to bring about Christian "unity."

In such a world of shifting powers, the sacrament of Penance stepped out of the ceremonial shadows of public symbol to become, at the bright Celtic margins of Christendom, a personal telling of a life with much at stake for the teller. The best kind of story.

How much of my life has been spent listening to stories. Curled up on the bulging springs of secondhand sofas, listening and trying to fathom the cads of my youth, the cads of my girlfriends' youths, this parental outrage, that lovers' quarrel. Now, sitting over ridiculously priced lattes in coffee shops that sell books and bookstores that, just as confusingly, sell coffee, I'm still sitting and listening. It's what friendship is to me—listening and telling stories, the first person voice buzzing away, sorting and contending, looking for meaning, looking for—I'm afraid—culprits.

Gossip, it's called. Feminists gleefully embraced the etymology of the word—God-speak—to polish the age-old feminine habit. Fine by me. But then, just as there was one single sin—*daydreaming*—in the "Examination of Conscience" at the back of the *Baltimore Catechism* that I refused to agree was a sin and imperiously threw out without a guilty pre–Vatican II backward glance, I never questioned the sweetness and goodness of gossip. It would be like questioning the taste of chocolate, the touch of silk.

What lay at the warm heart of all these stories was the sense of a real life at stake—it was the first person voice I loved. Not my own, even. But the voice of someone speaking out of the soul, that most breakable of vessels. I wasn't satisfied by the explanations and analyses of psychology. I wanted the pained voice itself rending itself with its story. I thought I was afraid of confession, of the little dark box of a place where I stammered out my sins, but really I wanted—and not just for myself, but for everyone with a burnt heart—a larger place where the tale could finally be told in all its shattering truth. I wanted the confessional voice, which I understood to be the intimate voice. I loved it when, in the nineteenth-century novels I began to read as a girl, the author—Thackeray, George Eliot—paused and addressed me. *Dear reader.* Yes! I'm listening, I wanted to cry back. I was listening for the story of the spirit, the inner story of experience. Which is another way of saying I was eager to hear the story of sin.

This spiritual storytelling began, of course, much earlier.

Augustine himself, who shocked his contemporaries not so much with his admission of lust but with his postconversion uncertainties, wrote his *Confessions* in 397, ten years after his Baptism. But even he, though an ancient, was baptized into the legitimized church and not into the outlaw church of the early martyrs. The Augustine of the *Confessions* is not—at least in voice and story— the Augustine of the sermons who fought to "reunite" the Catholic church. Today we see the *Confessions* of Augustine as nothing less than the first autobiography of the West, forever linking the confession of sin to the telling—and comprehending—of a life story.

It is impossible to think of confession—literary or sacramental— without drawing back to Augustine's great *confessio*. The fact that sex was indeed one of the real pulse points of his life and of his conversion may obscure the fact that the book is really about *thinking about oneself*. It is a passionate inquiry, in the form of a passionate prayer, into the formation of a life and consciousness. It is perhaps one of our impoverishments as moderns that we cannot hear the literary use of the word *confession* without reducing the enterprise to lurid goings-on, a sensational revelation of sordid affairs. The tale itself—the more salacious the better—is what we expect of a confession.

But the novelist Robert Clark in his memoir, *My Grandfather's House: A Geneology of Doubt and Faith*, hears the Latin *confessio* with the deeper resonance of his late medieval English ancestors. They might have translated *confessio* as "beknowing." It is a word lost to us, he says, "a little like our 'knowing' but with a reflexive twist: a knowing of one's knowing, in which we set what we think we know in front of us and step back from it." This is the wise "pondering in the heart" of the Virgin Mother in the Gospel.

It is the cusp between self and world, between action and reflection. Beknowing participates in the transitive ongoingness of a life being lived, but couples it with the essentially contemplative understanding of that living. Such knowing is the pivot point of penitence for it allows the sinner—the human being living a life—to regard, with the detachment necessary for remorse, the life that has gone awry.

For these late medieval Catholics, "the world," as Clark puts it, "was as real as the self, perhaps more real than the self, or at the very least co-extensive with it." As a result, his English ancestors "might have used the term 'beknowing' to describe what they did when they confessed their sins to the priest; and they might as easily have used it when they went back out into the hills of Suffolk to locate their sheep."

Beknowing is a giant step closer to the earth and its intelligence—and to the Celtic Christology of Patrick—than it is to Augustine's scrutinizing Christianity, arising out of a severe classical Platonism, with its nervous dualism dividing self and spirit. Yet in the *Confessions*, we have one of the most *beknowing* voices in Church history. Or maybe we have a writer who has found his true form: for in his autobiographical storytelling, not in the severe pronouncements of his heresy-sniffing theology, Augustine is alive and fascinating—and useful—to this day. He gave us the greatest model of beknowing that we have in spiritual writing, and he pondered with all the passion of his fierce intelligence. His is the great narrative examination of conscience of all time.

Beknowing and Mary's feminine "pondering" have about them a touch of the Renaissance daystar moment when individual consciousness seemed suddenly awakened and discovered that what it really wanted to do with itself, as Francis does in his "Canticle of the Creatures," was to praise, not blame. The claustrophobic shame the modern psychologized mind associates with "sin" and the cubicle of the confessional had not yet overwhelmed the self. The medieval world was a place of harsh retribution, of profoundly ingrained systems of control and hierarchy. But it was also a place to be forgiven in, that believed in its own system of absolution, that knew how to give itself a break while still maintaining a lively moral vision.

Maybe that's why pilgrimage was such a popular medieval form of expiation. Moving across the earth, close to the ground, in a small band of fellow penitents bearing the pilgrim scallop shell as their talisman, the sinners pondered their own life journey and listened to the tales of others along the way. In pondering—beknowing—his own story of sin, the pilgrim participated in an act neither wholly private nor entirely civic (and not legalistic). It was an outer penitence far removed from the ancient church's public penance. He—or she (remember the Wife of Bath, remember the Prioresse?)—was a self on a quest, enacting the immemorial metaphor that "life is a journey."

It is an eloquent coincidence that English narrative literature begins here, with Chaucer, amongst pilgrims who were, after all, penitents expiating—and retelling as stories—their sins (and the sins of others, of course: they, like my girlfriends and I, were great gossips). Here in the late medieval springtime, April is not yet the "cruellest month" of the alienated self. Though it is the painful season of Christ's agony and death, it belongs in Chaucer to the elemental happiness rising from the resurrecting earth:

Whan that Aprille with his shoures soote
The droghte of March hath perced to the roote,
And bathed every veyne in swich licour,
Of which vertu engendred is the flowr;
Whan Zephyrus eek with his sweete breeth
Inspired hath in every holt and heeth
The tendre croppes, and the yonge sonne
Hath in the Ram his halve cours yronne,
And smale foweles maken melodye
That slepen al the nyght with open ye
(So priketh hem nature in hir corages);
Thanne longen folk to goon on pilgrimages.

Sin, taken in the context of this metaphor of a spring journey, is an incident along the longer, larger Way. Penitence is a trip toward life. It even looks like fun—a bunch of people on vacation. Here, with the Renaissance winking on the horizon, the medieval penitent seems to have the best of both public and private penance: Sin needn't be a shaming public exposure, and expiation needn't be a private hairshirt, a half-step short of neurosis. Certainly pilgrimage as a form of expiation underscores the liberation that is meant to be at the core of the sacrament, the radiant lightness of the shriven heart.

This desire to be free "from all anxiety," as one of the blessings of the Mass puts it, is the oldest human spiritual hankering we have record of. The Psalmist knew its essential innerness even in the public life of a tribal culture. "Not burnt sacrifices you want, O Lord," he cries from the pathos of the private self struggling against the weight of public gestures. "Burnt offering you do not desire." What God wants is "a broken, contrite heart." This hidden, "broken" self is true and what God wants, not the "burnt sacrifices" in the public temple. Only the private voice can conduct the business of the inner world, no matter how much the civic authority wishes to control the individual as a member of the Mystical Body of Christ (or much later in post-industrial terms, as a cog in the machine). Augustine quotes the Psalms again and again in the *Confessions*, but never more tellingly than when, in Book VIII, he borrows the Psalmist's line, "I will sacrifice to Thee the sacrifice of praise." It is odd to think of sacrifice and praise being linked, to think of praise as sacrifice. Yet isn't praise of God the truest form of submission, and therefore of Penance?

In a way, the long history of the sacrament has been the history of the struggle between the need of the inner self to be unburdened and the requirement of the institution to have its members within its embrace (or clutch). The progression of its name changes—from Penance to Confession, and more recently to Reconciliation—bespeak this tension. Back and forth the pendulum goes, trying to balance this inevitable opposition of the soul and society. It is a chiaroscuro of the spirit, the light and dark of the self and the Church.

Without the inner satisfactions of forgiveness, the self is burdened beyond its capacity to carry on, to make the journey of its life. But who, exactly, does the forgiving? The medieval mind knew it was the Lord God, through his ordained representative, the priest. Modern psychology, on the other hand, demands that we forgive ourselves. This is meant to be a liberation (from the strictures of a confining institution), but it proves to be a ruinous burden for the lonely self.

The sacrament comes to us out of our deep past. It streams clouds of cultural assumptions from other, more communal, even tribal—and certainly hierarchical—times. It asks us to *receive* forgiveness, to see that it is a gift given, not an accomplishment of our own making.

The Twelve Steps of Alcoholics Anonymous, particularly the storytelling Steps 4 and 5 about "taking a personal inventory," make a fascinating modern secular side road of confession history. Much is made in AA of finding a relation with a "Higher Power." Many sobriety stories turn on the moment when the alcoholic, a confirmed atheist or agnostic (or someone who simply "isn't religious"), fastens (always in astonishment) on a serviceable Higher Power. This moment is almost never the blinding flash of insight associated with conversion to a belief in God— and the word *God*, of course, is expressly not used.

The Higher Power is often vaporish, or an absurd or apparently fanciful, even perverse, image that the alcoholic can somehow lean on (or look up to). This seemingly abstract term—Higher Power—bespeaks the contemporary secular squeamishness about a personal relation with God. But even more, it signals the contemporary commitment to the self over and above any mediating institution when it comes to the soul's business. The modern self will forgive itself, thank you very much. It is one of the many sly wisdoms of AA that it has found a way for the super-individualized self to find a secular conception of God.

In our own times, the self may be exhausted from what it is expected to be able to do for itself. The individual is asked to bear a lot of spiritual weight. The self cowers in the glare of its own celebrity. The contemporary world tells us we don't need absolution; we need understanding. Or rather, even more solipsistically, we need to understand ourselves. This is not the medieval beknowing of the pondering heart. It looks more like the modern client in a therapist's office, where the endless hunger of the spirit gets mixed up with the appeasable appetite of psychology, even though the gnawing sensation within won't go away, no matter how long you complain and explain, no matter how you try to fill up on words.

Although the Irish monks, according to Thomas Cahill, gave the Church the model of private confession, they were building on a yet earlier indigenous pattern—the Druid *anmchara*, the "soul-friend." This was a confidant chosen for life, an essential listener. As a well-known saying dating from pagan times in Ireland put it, "Anyone without a soul-friend is like a body without a head." The monks borrowed this pagan idea and deftly grafted it onto the sacrament of Penance, changing it forever.

At first it was a noncanonical procedure. Choosing one's

confessor in this early Irish form of confession was too personal to leave to the nearby priest, as if he were right for everyone. But of course over time this easy Irish custom of choosing the soul-friend from the randomness of life—man or woman, lay or ordained—was reined in by the Church. The soul-friend had to be an ordained priest, therefore of necessity a man. And given this canonical rigor, there was less a sense of a "friend" listening to one's sins. The priestly "confessor" became not only the anonymous absolver of sin, but a spiritual director.

Ignatius of Loyola, the founder of the Jesuits, was so beset with scruples about his sinfulness that he was close to suicide. His confessor ordered him not to confess anything unless it was a "very clear" sin. Unfortunately, this only exacerbated a case of acute scrupulosity because Ignatius thought *everything* passing through his mind was "very clear." But at least he had a confessor who was trying to befriend his overwrought soul, someone to save him from himself.

If the choice of confessor was restricted by the Church, the confessor in turn was bound by an even more harrowing regulation. The "seal of confession" was sacrosanct (according to Thomas Cahill, "it was practically the only sin the Irish considered unforgivable"). To disclose the testimony uttered within the confessional was—and remains—forbidden. The popular imagination adores the potential melodrama of this aspect of the sacrament, and in this century movies and TV have made delicious use of this moral imperative, a good priest refusing to divulge the name of a murderer, a bad priest—but no, oddly enough, there seem to be no popular examples of the priest who breaks the seal. We want to believe in the soul-friend.

The seal of the confessional has been adopted by psychotherapy and turned into the more lackluster concept of "confidentiality." This honor system of the therapeutic profession does not, of course, imperil the salvation of the therapist in the same way that the sacramental seal threatens the tattling priest.

There is even a patron saint of the confessional seal, Saint John Neponmuc. His statue is the most favored of all the saints lining the Charles Bridge in Prague. Tourists, in a ritual good luck gesture, have rubbed clean and bright his little bronze bas-relief image at the base of the statue. The scene depicts him in his famous martyr moment, bundled in a tarp as he is being tossed off the bridge in 1393 for staunchly refusing to divulge a secret the Bohemian Queen had confided to him in the confessional. Never mind that more recent historic documentation has established that this story is a pious fiction: The saint just had the bad luck of backing the wrong man as abbot in the deadly politicized religious atmosphere of his day.

The Church has always said that saints arise to highlight the needs of their particular times. Saint John Neponmuc, it appears, was in the right place—being dumped off the Charles Bridge—at the right time, just when the faithful needed dramatic evidence of the security safeguarding what was now an intensely private sacrament. He became the patron saint of confession, a mascot of priestly reliability. But he also became, inevitably, the patron saint of secrecy and therefore of isolation. With him, the modernity of the sacrament was established before modernity itself.

The little box, just big enough to hold a single kneeling penitent, became the dark sanctuary of the self, the one safe place. This closet of privacy, the waking modern mind decided, was worth dying for.

Bless me, Father, it has been thirty years—make that thirty-two—since my last confession.... An absurd way to begin. But when, a few years ago, I returned to the sacrament, I might have said something like that. Might have—but didn't. But I thought it; the old formula beginning of confessional recitation is bred deep inside a pre–Vatican II mind.

Maybe because of that association, I had let the sacrament "lapse"—another old-style Catholic term. Confession belonged to the bad old Church, not the one I was trying to be part of. *My* Church was "progressive," and its allegiance to tradition and to ancient liturgy were also, in their self-conscious ways, progressive too. I didn't stand in line in the basement of St. Luke's anymore, I didn't seek out the solemn drama of the little black box. And most of all, I didn't present my grocery list of sins. I let the congregational ritual of Reconciliation, communal and not sin-specific, take care of the confession department of Catholic life.

And of course I went into therapy, huddling for months of weekly "sessions," "dealing with" what I learned to call "my issues," sorting out the litter of a life at what felt like the midpoint. I shared a couch in a room full of green plants with my therapist's elderly springer, who regarded me with his baleful spaniel eyes before sighing deeply and rounding into his corner of the couch where he slept the sleep of the blameless for the entire hour, moaning occasionally, whether from dreams of misery or delight, it was not clear. The couch was slung so low that I felt I was rising from a crouch when I finally left at the end of my hour, rudely awakening the dog as I heaved myself up and out.

I went every week. I told my tale. I told it this way. Then I told it that way. I was balled up in a passionate determination to "fig-ure things out." Sometimes I blamed *him,* sometimes *her.* There were plenty of hims and hers to work over. But inevitably, of course, I blamed myself. It was a completely absorbing enterprise for perhaps eighteen months, and at the same time I marveled at the boredom of it, the tedium of my telling. But how could I be bored? This was my life!

It wasn't a grocery list of sins. But it was, in a way, even less compelling because something was flattening the narrative. At least a list has its clean purpose, nothing more, nothing less than its gathered details. But in my storytelling there was a desperate wish that made my testimony unreliable. I didn't see this for a long time. I kept talking. But finally, as if the tumblers of a com-plicated lock had finally come round in the magical right combi-nation, I got the message: I was never going to figure it out. To my greater surprise I registered this fact with pleasure, with a sense of liberation.

My therapist congratulated me: I was done with therapy. The springer spaniel didn't even cock an eye open when I slipped from the couch and left the room full of green plants behind.

Shortly after this, I went on a retreat to a monastery perched high on a mountain above the Pacific, the steep slant of the hillocky land ending in the great pastel muddle of sky and sea.

Some days it was impossible to find the horizon, the air and water had conspired so successfully to confuse themselves. The days began before dawn with Lauds in the chapel. Every day was silent except for our mouthing the Psalmist's ancient passions, his cries for mercy, his rebukes and terrors, his lyric tendernesses. Such moodiness at the heart of Western religion!

The monks, who dressed in casual clothes around the monastery grounds, wore cream-colored robes in the chapel which, strangely enough, accentuated their individuality rather than obscuring it. One day, toward the end of my week on the mountain, I realized I had settled on a face I wished to make my confession to. The lean and abstract face of an elderly monk. I hadn't even realized I had been looking for a confessor, but there he was. He seemed startled when I asked him if he would hear my confession, but he agreed immediately.

We met later that day in a room at the side of the chapel. He was wearing blue jeans and a plaid flannel shirt. I had expected the cream-colored robe. But as he sat down in a straight-back chair, he produced a hand-woven stole and draped it around his shoulders. And instantly became a priest, and the setting, sacramental. I sat in a similar chair facing him. The room was large and airy. He smiled as I looked around. "I suppose you're used to doing this in the box," he said with a gentle irony that referred not to me, it seemed, but to the world we both had once inhabited and which, he intimated with his smile, I was braving again.

I told him I didn't even know what confession was anymore. I knew this admission wouldn't faze him. I produced the little St.

Luke's-style grocery list I had prepared. We both smiled over it. "Maybe you should just talk a little," he said.

But I didn't tell my tale. I told him what I wished for, the qualities of heart I lacked and wished were mine. The sacrament, he said, as if to himself though I was aware I had been listened to with absolute attention, is not really about sin. It is about hardness of heart. It was a scriptural term, he reminded me— *hardness of heart*; it referred to the ball of pride and fear and misery that makes freedom so difficult. The sacrament, he said, is about freedom.

I talked. He listened. There was absolutely no disapproval for anything I said. He radiated a quiet, absorbed *interest* in my sins. Like a doctor looking at a symptom, trying to find cause and cure. He had a perfect pitch of warmth and coolness. We were meeting in a free middle, between friendship and being utter strangers. It was sacred ground, impersonal, sacramental. It was almost casual, like sitting in a boat on one of the lost inland Minnesota lakes with my father, waiting for a nibble. Together in the stillness of the natural world, knowing the truth was down there and might bite, might be mine. But there was nothing to do, just put yourself in the presence of it and see what happens.

He suggested I read the whole Gospel of Luke for my penance. "Take six months—don't rush." Then he smiled. "Seeing you've been away from the sacrament so long, you can afford a long penance." He wasn't toying with me. He was playing with the form. An artist.

He raised his hand over my bowed head, said the ancient absolving words I knew from Latin: *te absolvo. . . .* Then we parted, he to the monastery, I to the mountain where I stood alone in the late afternoon light, looking out at the rind of America as it peels off into the flourish of the sea, the sky somewhere out there in it all too. *The sacrament is not really about sin. It is about hardness of heart. . . .*

The burnt sacrifices of self-castigation, of blame and shame, all the slaughters on the high altar of the self that it is possible to present as one's truth. It is a modern form of hard-heartedness, earnest but rigid. A sentence formed in my head—though it felt as if it came not from me but out of the damp air drenched with the smell of eucalyptus: *You don't get to understand; you just get to acquiesce.*

The black box had opened, its dank closet revealed itself now as nothing less than the panorama of the glorious world. I stood there, shivering in the growing cold, unable to make out the hinge of sea and sky, glad of that confusion, glad to give over to the mystery at last.

SOURCES

Maria Boulding, O.S.B., translator, *The Confessions of St. Augustine,* (New York: Vintage, 1998).

Peter Brown, *Augustine of Hippo* (Los Angeles and Berkeley: University of California Press, 1969).

Thomas Cahill, *How the Irish Saved Civilization* (New York: Doubleday, 1995).

Robert Clark, *My Grandfather's House: A Geneology of Doubt and Faith* (New York: Picador, 1999).

Michael Downey, *Clothed in Christ: The Sacraments and Christian Living* (New York: Crossroad, 1987).

Peter E. Fink, S.J., editor, *The New Dictionary of Sacramental Worship* (Collegeville, MN: Liturgical Press, 1990).

Frank O'Connor, "My First Confession," from *Collected Stories* (New York: Random House, 1982).

Michael Steinmen, *Frank O'Connor at Work* (Syracuse, NY: Syracuse University Press, 1990).

EUCHARIST

RON HANSEN

I first received Christ in the Eucharist in 1955. It was December 8th, the feast of Mary's Immaculate Conception, and my brother Rob and I were celebrating our eighth birthday. And because of that, or because we were such goshdarn cute twins, we were given the honor of leading the sixty-child procession of second graders to the altar rail of Holy Angels Church, in Omaha. We wore new shoes, navy blue slacks, white shirts with red cufflinks, and white clip-on ties. We'd slicked down our hair with Wildroot Creme Oil. We felt spiffy.

I have no recollection of the Mass or of the homily preached by Monsignor Patrick Aloysius Flanagan, the younger brother of Boys Town's founder. But my memory is helped by Kodachrome snapshots that were taken of our procession toward the high altar, our hands folded and fingers steepled, our faces solemn, reverent, and way on the other side of cool and insouciant. We'd been catechized to feel awe for the mystery of Christ's presence in the sacrament we'd receive, but we'd heard from older kids on the playground that the Host tasted horrible and Rob was afraid he'd hate it and yet be punished with hellfire if he spit it out. And I was full of childish wonder about the changes Jesus would make in me. Would I be a Superman, a holy man, a healer? Would homework now be easier? Would I be a wiz? Or would I be jailed in piety, condemned to sinlessness, obedience, and no fun?

We knelt at a polished marble altar railing and, lest the Blessed Sacrament fall onto our unconsecrated hands, hid them under the drapery of a railing-long linen cloth. I peeked at Monsignor Flanagan sidling along, holding up the Host to my classmates as he recited Latin and laid the thin round wafer on their tongues.

Then Monsignor was in front of me in his gold-embroidered white vestments, a seemingly towering figure, as stern and intimidating as the destroying God of Abraham. I felt the cold touch of the paten against my throat as a cynical eighth grade altar boy in black cassock and white surplice held it under my chin, and with humility and childish worry I stuck out my drying tongue like a toddler being fed from a spoon. Watching the Host, I heard Monsignor say as he made the sign of the cross with it, *"Corpus Dómini nostri Jesu Christi custódiat ánimam tuam in vitam aetérnam. Amen."* May the Body of our Lord Jesus Christ preserve your soul into life everlasting. So be it. And in spite of my unworthiness, he gave me First Communion.

I hesitated, then stood, huddling a little as I walked back to my pew under the smiles of my father and mother and the ever-wary gaze of Sister Mary Evans, my second grade teacher—still feeling the wafer like plastic on the roof of my mouth, but not disliking the taste. Then I knelt heedfully upright and mentally prayed as we'd been instructed to do, some scared and scientific part of me assaying myself for chemical reactions or a sudden infusion of wisdom while fancying Christ now sitting dismally in my scoundrel soul, my oh so many sins pooling like sewer water at his sandaled feet. But soon I saw that I was still me; there would be no howls of objection, no immediate correction or condemnation, no hint that I was under new management, just the calming sense that whoever I was was fine with Jesus.

It was a grace I hadn't imagined.

The first Jewish followers of the Way of Jesus of Nazareth primarily evangelized other Jews like themselves, just as their Messiah had, but soon took the good news of the life and teachings of Jesus to Gentiles, and for those non-Jews translated *b'rakhah*, the Hebrew word for "blessing," with the Greek word *eucharistia*, or "thanksgiving." And so, though the word *Eucharist* is never used in the New Testament, it became by association the common name for what Catholics call the Mass.

The first writing of any sort to mention Christ's Last Supper is Paul's first letter to the Corinthians, sent in the year 54:

> For I received from the Lord what I also handed on to you, that the Lord Jesus on the night when he was betrayed took a loaf of bread, and when he had given thanks, he broke it and said, "This is my body that is for you. Do this in remembrance of me." In the same way he took the cup also, after

supper, saying, "This cup is the new covenant in my blood. Do this, as often as you drink it, in remembrance of me." For as often as you eat this bread and drink the cup, you proclaim the Lord's death until he comes. (I Cor. 11:23–26)

Twenty to thirty years later, the evangelists Mark, Matthew, and Luke developed their own, non-eyewitness accounts of Christ's last Passover meal in their gospels, interpreting an inherited Aramaic tradition that the first generation of Christians thought was faithful to what Jesus actually said and did on that Thursday night.

In the liturgical practice of the Catholic church the first three gospel accounts have been conflated into one text:

The day before he suffered
he took bread into his sacred hands
and looking up to heaven,
to you, his almighty Father,
he gave you thanks and praise.
He broke the bread,
gave it to his disciples, and said:
Take this, all of you, and eat it:
this is my body which will be given up for you.
When supper was ended,
he took the cup.
Again he gave you thanks and praise,
gave the cup to his disciples, and said:
Take this, all of you, and drink from it:
this is the cup of my blood,

the blood of the new and everlasting covenant.
It will be shed for you and for all
so that sins may be forgiven.
Do this in memory of me.

Everlasting covenant. Religious Jews had, and have, far stronger associations with the word *covenant* than most Christians do, for it was their forefathers' hardwon covenant with God that formed them into a nation, and fidelity to that covenant was the overriding concern of their religious, social, and national existence.

In biblical times to remember meant not only to recall to mind whatever had been done by God but also to effectively experience it again, to have the past authentically present. Remembering, the Jews would be conscious of God's intervention in their history and, in gratitude for that, be called to holy action now.

And so it was with the apostles. Hearing Christ's words at the Last Supper, they would have harkened back to the Exodus when Moses mediated the covenant between God and the Israelite tribes, forming them into one people, concluding and sealing the promise with the blood of slaughtered animals, and celebrating its enactment with a feast. (Exod. 24:4–11) Only after Christ's crucifixion and resurrection, however, would the apostles have seen that Christ had offered *himself* as a sacrifice and mediated a *new* covenant of salvation for them. The letter to the Hebrews puts it this way: "But when Christ came as a high priest . . . he entered once for all into the Holy Place, not with the blood of goats and calves, but with his own blood, thus obtaining eternal redemption." (Heb. 9:11–12)

With the feast of Passover (otherwise known as the feast of *matzah*, unleavened bread) the Jews commemorated God's great act of salvation in "passing over" their own homes—so signified with the blood of a lamb—as the firstborn sons of the Egyptians were slain. They commemorated, too, the flight of the Israelites from Egypt after four hundred years of slavery; their passage through the Sea of Reeds; the sealing of the covenant at Sinai; and their final conquest of Canaan, the foretold land of milk and honey.

In the time of Christ, the feast could only be celebrated in Jerusalem. Just before sundown on the fourteenth day of Nisan, the first month of the year, lambs were slaughtered in the Temple by the heads of households, and high priests poured out the collected blood at the foot of the altar of sacrifice. Jesus, as the highest ranking member of a *chaburah*, or brotherhood, would have fulfilled the functions of the head of household and ritually killed and roasted the lamb, then carried it to a festive and illuminated upper room, *kataluma* in Greek—the same word that is generally translated as "inn" in the narrative of Christ's birth. The Jerusalem *kataluma* was, according to the gospel of Luke, furnished with soft, pillowed couches horseshoed around a low table so that the guests could recline on the brace of their left elbows and have their right hands free for eating. The format was not only that of a Seder and a hospitality meal welcoming those on a journey, but also that of a Hellenistic symposium, or a convivial intellectual conversation nurtured by wine. According to the gospel of John, in this meal the focus of conversation was a farewell discourse by Jesus.

We know from his criticism of Simon the Pharisee (Luke 7:44–46) that Jesus valued the Jewish customs associated with the gracious hosting of a meal, so we can presume that in his role as host of the feast of *Pesach* (*Pascha* in Greek), Jesus would have kissed his guests in greeting them, anointed their heads with perfumed oil, and as we see in the gospel of John, washed their feet, just as slaves did then. Commencing the feast, Jesus would have first offered a prayer of thanksgiving to bless the fruit of the vine and then passed the cup, or chalice, of wine to his friends to share. Then the flat cakes of unleavened *matzah*—the so-called bread of affliction—would have been served along with a kind of leek, *maror*, that was dipped in a dish of salted water and vinegar. After that the lamb would have been brought to the table.

Many believe it's possible that John, the beloved disciple, was just a boy then, and it would have been he who asked the host, "Why is this night different from all other nights?" and Jesus would have recited the *haggadah*, or narrative of the memorial rite, recalling the events of the Exodus: "We were slaves of Pharaoh in Egypt and the Eternal, our God, brought us out from there with a strong hand and an outstretched arm. Now if God had not brought out our forefathers from Egypt, then even we, our children, and our children's children might still have been enslaved to Pharaoh in Egypt."

With the pouring of a second cup of wine, Jesus would have continued the remembrance—in liturgical terms, the *anamnesis*—concluding it with praise of the Eternal God in what Jews call the Great Hallel: Psalms 114 and 115:1–8. All who were there would have then shared the wine and finished eating the *matzah* and lamb and, perhaps, stewed fruit. Jesus would have blessed a third cup of wine with the second half of the Hallel, singing a hymn made up of Psalms 115:9–18, 116, and 117. The feast would have ended just around midnight. And then, the gospels tell us, Jesus and his disciples went to a garden across the Kidron Valley from Jerusalem, on the hill of the Mount of Olives, in order to continue their prayer.

With about fifteen other classmates, Rob and I became altar boys in sixth grade. There were no altar girls then, and we were not acolytes, as in other religious denominations, for in Roman Catholicism with its hints, always, of incense and cowls and medieval cathedrals, the acolyte designation formally belongs just below that of deacon and is the highest ranking of the four minor orders, above exorcist, lector, and ostiary (or doorkeeper).

To become an altar boy, we'd had to pass an oral exam on the pronunciation and memorization of the Latin of the Tridentine Rite on a four-page booklet of Mass responses, and a walk-through exam on our suave reverence in serving the priest: genuflecting to Christ in the tabernacle without tilting or grunting, shifting the Roman Missal from the epistle side to the gospel side of the altar with such effortless silence that the book seemed to have been spirited there, trickling wine into the chalice at the Offertory with all the seriousness of a sommelier at a four-star restaurant, ringing the handbells at the Consecration for just the length of a Jesus, Mary, and Joseph.

At that jaunty and guileless age I had no inkling of the queasy stage fright I'd feel at my first weekday 6:30 A.M. Mass when I walked out to the high altar in my cassock and surplice with an older altar boy and the holy terror of Monsignor Flanagan, nor of the seeming thirty-minute agony of reciting in halting and arduous Latin my first *"Confiteor,"* nor of the fear and panic that would roost in my chest as I failed to predict one after another of the Monsignor's extremely particular expectations.

At the *"Hanc igitur,"* when it was time for the Consecration, we two servers humbly ascended the three plush, carpeted steps of the high altar to kneel beside Monsignor Flanagan, the older boy on the right side handling the ringing of four joined bells. The red-lettered rubrics of the Sacramentary called for the priest to pronounce the words of Consecration, genuflect, adore the Host for a moment, rise, elevate the Host for all the congregation behind him to see, replace it on the paten, and genuflect once again. We held the hem of his knee-length chasuble so Monsignor could do all that without interference. I was wholly focused on doing it right, and grateful that I wasn't also in charge of ringing the bells, when the old white-haired priest hunched forward and, holding the Host in his index fingers and thumbs, slowly, softly, and reverently recited the Latin translation of Christ's words at the Last Supper, *"Hoc est enim Corpus meum."* For this is my Body. And a little later, Monsignor hunched over the tilted chalice, speaking into it as he slowly and scrupulously recited, *"Hic est enim Calix Sánguinis mei, novi et ætérni testaménti: mystérium fidei: qui pro vobis et pro multis effundítur in remissiónem peccatórum."* For this is the Chalice of my Blood of the new and eternal covenant: the mystery of faith: which shall be shed for you and for many unto the forgiveness of sins. *"Hæc quotiescúmque fecéritis, in mei memóriam faciétis."* As often as you shall do these things, in memory of Me shall you do them.

I was in awe. My theology of the Real Presence was that of a sixth grader, and my Latin was in its infancy, so large parts of the history and lore of the sacrament were going way over my head, but I felt privileged to be there and observe from up close the mystery in which Christ's body and blood were somehow actually confected from ordinary bread and wine. If my own faith had not confirmed the fact of that event, Monsignor Flanagan's faith in it surely would have. *All you have heard,* he seemed to be saying, *is true.*

And when on other days I would glimpse Monsignor in the priest's sacristy before Mass, kneeling with arthritic pain on his prie-dieu, and solemnly adoring Christ in the tabernacle, I would understand that if it *was* all true, if Jesus was really there, you'd be insolent and vain to do other than what the old priest so reverently did.

In Luke's gospel, the life of Jesus is full of journeys in which he is dependent on the hospitality of friends and strangers for his food and lodging. Even at his birth, Jesus was laid in a manger— the trough in a barn from which cattle feed—because there was no room for the holy family in an inn. Thirty years later, during his public ministry, as Jesus and his disciples were walking toward a village, Luke writes that a voice cried out, " 'I will follow you wherever you go.' And Jesus said to him, 'Foxes have holes, and birds of the air have nests; but the Son of Man has nowhere to lay his head.' " (Luke 9:57–58) Jesus was frankly and unashamedly dependent on the graciousness of others, and fulfilled to perfection the highly choreographed customs of ancient hospitality by which a stranger gradually becomes a guest.

Ten meals are featured in Luke's gospel. There is the banquet at the house of Levi, where Pharisees complain that Jesus is eating and drinking with tax collectors and sinners, and he answers, "I have come to call not the righteous but sinners to repentance." (Luke 5:32) There is a dinner with the Pharisee named Simon, at which a notorious woman weeps at the feet of Jesus, dries his feet with her hair, finds reconciliation, and inspires the parable of the forgiving creditor who was loved most by the one whose debt was largest.

In the third meal, at "a deserted place" in Bethsaida, Luke hints at associations with the Sinai experience of Israel's flight from Egypt as he tells how Jesus miraculously fed five thousand using a eucharistic formula that in Luke's time would have been familiar to all Christians: "And taking the five loaves and two fish, he looked up to heaven, and blessed and broke them, and gave them to the disciples to set before the crowd. And all ate and were filled." (Luke 9:16–17)

On a journey to Jerusalem, Jesus is apparently alone when he visits the home of an unmarried woman named Martha—a scandalous act in those times. There Martha's sister Mary sits at his feet as if she were his student, an impudence for females then, as is seen when Martha insists Jesus tell her sister to help with the serving, *diakonia*—the term Luke will use for ministry to the community in Acts. Jesus immediately assesses the actual cause of Martha's anxiety; it is not that she is taxed with many household chores but that she's neglected the one thing that would give meaning to her service, which is being in his presence and hearing his wisdom.

In the next chapter, Jesus is invited to a noon meal at the home of a Pharisee whose strict interpretation of Jewish law incites him to shame Jesus for failing to carry out the formalities of hand-washing and purification of cup and dish before he sat to eat. Jesus responds by indicting as hypocrites those Pharisees and scholars of the law who concentrate on the ostentations of religion while simultaneously ignoring religion's call to justice for others and a full and abiding love of God.

The host at his next meal is a Pharisee of greater importance, the featured guests are scribes and lawyers, and the dinner, which seems to be a formal Hellenistic symposium, is being held on the Sabbath. All there watch Jesus closely and are offended when on a holy day Jesus heals a man with dropsy, an effusion of fluid into the skin and muscle tissues that causes painful swelling. Jesus counters their feelings of insult with parables that focus on the shared meal as a fulfillment of the purpose of the Sabbath—that is, to nourish health and hope and solidarity with the poor, the lame, the blind, the oppressed, and all who hear the word of God and act on it.

Concern for justice and the poor is also highlighted in the story of hospitality in the house of Zacchaeus, the chief tax collector in Jericho and a wealthy man short in stature. Wanting to see the famous prophet he thinks of as Lord, but held far off by the crowds, Zacchaeus scrabbles up a sycamore tree, but is soon called down by Jesus, who says it is necessary for him to be Zacchaeus's houseguest, meaning that in his stay with Zacchaeus Jesus will fulfill his mission of offering salvation to sinners, " 'for the Son of Man has come to seek and save what was lost.' " (Luke 19:10)

Reading over these stories I have been struck by how wanting in fun and food and relaxation these dinners seemed to be. Jesus is constantly quizzed or critiqued or compelled to act as a mediator in our gospel accounts, but there must have been thousands of meals with friends and hospitable strangers during his three-year public ministry, dinners filled with graciousness, good food and wine, and maybe even hilarity. There are jests and puns and comic situations throughout the New Testament—Christ's dealings with his enemies are never without irony or wordplay—but there is also a grimness in the evangelists that probably has its origins in the persecutions that the first-century Christians were undergoing.

And so it is sometimes necessary for me to remember noontime dinners on Sundays. Eight A.M. Mass would be just a memory and the Omaha *World-Herald* would be scattered about the living room as we sat down to my mother's pot roast, boiled potatoes, and canned vegetables, or chicken, green vegetables, mashed potatoes, and salty gravy. Cake, pie, or canned fruit cocktail for dessert. Dad would retell comic incidents from his job as an electrical engineer for the Omaha Public Power District. My three older sisters or Rob would talk about what our teachers said at school, or what chums did to annoy them, or what their schemes were for the afternoon. Mom would talk about the content of phone calls or letters she'd gotten from old friends or relatives. Reaching for a second helping, I'd probably spill my glass of milk. And in that serene, good-natured, *Ozzie and Harriet* setting we each got a sense of where we'd been, who we were, and what we hoped to become. It gave us our identity, not just as a family of two parents and five children, but as unique individuals within that grouping.

Jesus was doing that in all his meals, singling out his hosts and guests as highly individual children of God, admonishing, praising, or helping them as they needed, and yet generalizing in ways that are instructive to us even today. And that is never more true than in his ascent to Jerusalem where the fundamental themes of the seven previous meals are remembered and combined in the stunning climax of his Last Supper. There a new Paschal mystery is introduced, that of Christ "passing over" to his Father and redeeming creation through his life, death, resurrection, ascension, and exaltation. As presented in Luke, the supper is a liturgical event in which Christ offers thanksgiving to God and shares the *matzah* with his friends, connecting those actions—through the metonymy "body"—with the affliction he will suffer on the cross. In like manner Christ offers thanksgiving and shares the cup of wine, connecting those actions with the blood he will shed and the blood of the new covenant foretold more than six hundred years earlier by the prophet Jeremiah:

> The days are surely coming, says the LORD, when I will make a new covenant with the house of Israel and the house of Judah. . . . I will put my law within them, and I will write it

on their hearts; and I will be their God, and they shall be my people. No longer shall they teach one another, or say to each other, "Know the LORD," for they shall all know me, from the least of them to the greatest, says the LORD; for I will forgive their iniquity, and remember their sin no more. (Jer. 31:31–34)

The first seven meals featured Jesus as prophet. At the Last Supper, Jesus asserted by word and symbol that he was the *Mashiach*, the Christ, and commanded his apostles to share similar meals in memorial of his life, passion, and resurrection, in such a way making Christ truly present again as sacrifice, redeemer, and Lord. Celebrated worthily, with faith in the power of the Holy Spirit, that memorial would be a sacrament in which Christ himself would be at work, healing and transforming others and uniting them to himself.

There would be two other, post-resurrection meals in Luke, the first of them in Emmaus, seven miles from Jerusalem, with a disciple named Cleopas and another unnamed disciple, possibly his wife. Each was probably to become an elder, *presbyteros,* in the early church. Confused by reports of the resurrection, Cleopas and the other disciple were heatedly discussing the amazing things that had gone on since the feast of *Pesach,* when they were joined on the road by a sojourner to Jerusalem. He at first seemed in the dark about the crucifixion of Jesus and the shock of his rising from the dead, but then the stranger called them foolish for their failure to understand the significance of the Passion, and interpreted the Torah and all the prophets for them as a way of explaining why Jesus had to die. Their hearts on fire due to his inspiring teaching, they invited the man to stay with them in Emmaus and there, offering the *b'rakhah*, he broke the *matzah* and handed it to them, and they finally realized their guest was Jesus himself. And then he became invisible to them.

In their excitement Cleopas and the other disciple hurried back to Jerusalem to inform the huddled Eleven of what Jesus had said and done, and the risen Jesus appeared there as well, calming those who were frightened that he was a ghost by showing them his injured hands and feet. "While in their joy they were disbelieving and wondering, he said to them, 'Have you anything to eat?' They gave him a piece of broiled fish, and he took it and ate in their presence." (Luke 24:41–43) That was the tenth and final meal, for afterward Jesus blessed them and ascended to heaven.

The Jesus who was symbolic food at his birth, lying with straw in a manger, or cattle trough, is later seen sharing food with others throughout his public ministry, becomes real food and wine at his Last Supper, and in his final meeting with his apostles was teaching them to feed and serve others. And in blessing them he was fulfilling God's two-thousand-year-old promise to Abraham, that in his offspring all the families on earth would be blessed.

Were I asked for a shorthand version of what the Mass is, I need do no more than quote the lyrics of a song by Marty Haugen: "We remember how you loved us to your death, and still we celebrate for you are with us here. And we believe that we will see you when you come in your glory, Lord. We remember, we celebrate, we believe."

The first Jewish converts to the Way of Christ did that as well, for in Luke's Acts of the Apostles we find: "They devoted themselves to the apostles' teaching and fellowship, to the breaking of bread and the prayers.... Day by day, as they spent much time together in the temple, they broke bread at home and ate their food with glad and generous hearts, praising God and having the goodwill of all the people." (Acts 2:42–47)

In the instructions on "the way of life" in the *Didache* of the late first century, a strong Judaic heritage can be seen in the blessings of the first eucharistic celebrations:

> Now about the Eucharist: This is how to give thanks. First in connection with the cup:
>
> We thank you, our Father, for the holy vine of David, your child, which you have revealed through Jesus, your child [servant]. To you be glory forever.
>
> Then in connection with the broken bread:
>
> We thank you, our Father, for life and knowledge which you have revealed through Jesus, your child. To you be glory forever.

Writing to Emperor Antoninus Pius in 155, Justin Martyr tried to explain Christian practices, giving us a fascinating portrait of how liturgical—and familiar—their celebrations had become in just fifty years.

> On the day we call the day of the sun, all who dwell in the city or country gather in the same place. The memoirs of the

apostles and the writings of the prophets are read, as much as time permits. When the reader has finished, he who presides over those gathered admonishes and challenges them to imitate these beautiful things. Then we all rise together and offer prayers for ourselves . . . and for all others, wherever they may be, so that we may be found righteous by our life and actions, and faithful to the commandments, so as to obtain eternal salvation. When the prayers are concluded we exchange the kiss. Then someone brings bread and a cup of water and wine mixed together to him who presides over the brethren. He takes them and offers praise and glory to the Father of the universe, through the name of the Son and of the Holy Spirit and for a considerable time he gives thanks that we have been judged worthy of these gifts. When he has concluded the prayers and thanksgiving, all present give voice to an acclamation by saying: "Amen." When he who presides has given thanks and the people have responded, those whom we call deacons give to those present the "eucharisted" bread, wine and water and take them to those who are absent.

Christ's encounter with Cleopas and the unnamed disciple on the journey to Emmaus—interpreting Scripture for them and blessing, breaking, and sharing the bread—had provided second-century Christians with the structure for a eucharistic ritual that is still fundamentally the same after nearly two thousand years.

We still assemble on Sundays in a church or home for a gathering at which Christ himself presides in the person of a bishop or priest. Introductory prayers and a penitential rite collect us as one, acquaint us with the season or feast, and prepare us for the

Liturgy of the Word. In Christ's time a service in the synagogue called for two readings from the scrolls and the singing of a psalm, and so it is that we read an extract from the Hebrew scriptures and from the epistles, and a psalm and Alleluia are sung, and then we hear a gospel account of the life of Jesus, the fulfillment of God's word. A homily or instruction is followed by a confession of faith, usually the Nicene Creed, and a series of intercessory prayers of Jewish origin, for the needs of the Church, the nation, the locality, the persecuted, the sick, or those who have died.

The Liturgy of the Eucharist recalls the four verbs of the institution narratives: Jesus took, blessed, broke, gave. In this, the former Canon of the Mass, we begin with what used to be called the Offertory, in which Christians unite their own lives with Christ's life and ministry in the self-offering of their words and deeds in the gifts of bread and wine. Receiving the gifts, the priest articulates the faith and action of the congregation in offering thanksgiving to God with a variation on the *Kiddush*, a Jewish blessing, and after some preparatory rites commences the great eucharistic prayer by which the Church is created, enacted, and characterized. The prayer is introduced by one of ninety-one prefaces for various liturgical seasons and feasts, which is concluded with the *Sanctus*, the "Holy, holy, holy" that greeted Jesus on his final entrance to Jerusalem. The preface is followed by the *epiclesis*, or solemn invocation of the Holy Spirit on the gifts; the Consecration, or narrative of Christ's institution of this memorial at the Last Supper; and the *anamnesis*, or the act of remembrance that makes Christ's actions present and invites the faithful to recall their own crucifixions and resurrections. In communion with the worldwide Church, we then join in a memorial prayer, interceding for all Christians living and dead, that they may find light, happiness, and peace in the presence of God, through Christ "from whom all good things come."

The Doxology, a hymn of praise to the Holy Trinity, concludes the great eucharistic prayer and leads into the Communion Rite where the faithful first recite "The Lord's Prayer," recalling that we are one family with God as our Father, and then we offer each other a handshake, hug, or kiss as a sign of peace, unity, intimacy, and love. Tertullian called it "the seal of prayer." The Host or bread is broken in the "fraction rite" and shared, as at a family meal, when the congregation goes forward to the banquet table, as on their journey to the heavenly kingdom, and receive in faith the body and blood of Christ.

Catholic theology teaches that sacraments effect what they signify, and so it is here. Our gifts of bread and wine are changed by Christ from being symbols of ourselves and our self-giving, to being Christ himself and his self-giving. They are no longer things; they are God. And in this extravagant gift of the Eucharist we are, as Saint Augustine wrote, receiving ourselves, for our Baptism formed us into the body of Christ and his members. Our "Amen," our "So be it," is a sign that we are both receiving and giving, that Christ has not just become present to us, but that we have become present to Christ. The liturgical celebration is concluded after silent prayer of adoration, gratitude, and petition, and we are sent out as Christ's disciples to love and serve God and one another, with a blessing in the name of the Father, and of the Son, and of the Holy Spirit.

With Constantine the Great's miraculous conversion to Christianity in the year 312, he altered, for good and ill, the nature of the church of Rome. Rather than being a contrarian, Mediterranean religion, it became worldwide and, at its worst, imperialist. Rather than being persecuted, it was now legally sanctioned, privileged, increasingly wealthy, but shackled by its too cozy alliance with the interests and intrigues of monarchies. And churches themselves took on that royal character, becoming as grand as palaces, as opulent as theaters, with magnificent paintings and ornate altars positioned like high thrones, and with rood screens and communion railings to hold the laity at bay. Christ's instruction to Mary Magdalene just after his resurrection, *"Nolo me tangere,"* don't touch me, was used continually as a theme in art to school the masses in a needed separation between the ordained and the not. The liturgy of the Eucharist was no longer an action of the assembly but the sole and private action of a priest whose back was to them so that he could face Christ the King in the tabernacle and concentrate on confecting the sacrament in whispered secrecy. To the illiterate and generally uncatechized masses, it was no less than magic and sorcery; and they watched with a mixture of gratitude and wonder as the priest interceded for them and inveigled a seemingly judgmental and damning God out of heaven and into their midst with the Latin words of consecration they misheard as "hocus-pocus." Reception of Communion by the laity became so rare and their theology so childish that it was possible to bruit about the old wives' tale that the Host would bleed if scratched.

The Reformation was a protest against such a church, one that in a millennium of chaotic growth and political chicanery had become shoddy, disorderly, disreputable, and adrift from its biblical roots. Even as it condemned the Reformation, the Council of Trent—which met intermittently in Trento, Italy, between 1545 and 1563—did much to address the grievances that made Protestantism inevitable and the council necessary. It disciplined the financial dealings of the Roman Curia, inaugurated rigorous standards for priestly formation in seminaries, determined the meaning and number of the sacraments, and with the call for the publication of a *Missal Romanum*, homogenized the liturgy of the Mass, which had theretofore as many variations in the West as there were countries where it was celebrated.

Clarifying its position in contradistinction to many Protestant sects, the Council of Trent also declared that Christ sacrifices himself in the Mass just as he did on the cross, and through Christ, our immolated victim and priest, the Mass itself becomes an unbloody sacrifice of praise, thanksgiving, and commemoration, through which the merits of Christ's redeeming death are applied to the souls of the living and the dead for the expiation of sin. And Trent made it official Catholic teaching that in the consecrated elements of bread and wine, Christ is not just a spiritual presence, but a real one; that in the Eucharist the elements were transubstantiated into Christ's body and blood to such a degree that nothing of the bread and wine remained beyond what metaphysicians call accidentals.

The city of Trento was called Tridentum in ancient times, so the Latin liturgy of its *Roman Missal* came to be called the Tridentine Mass. Erring on the side of inclusion, embellishment, redundancy, and piety, the Missal prescribed as necessities those ancillary prayers, such as the prologue to John's gospel, that may have been part of the private devotions of ministers in some countries. Even when a choir chanted a text, the priest was required to secretly recite it, as if the song of the unordained would not be heard by God. But there was a dignity, grandness, and pageantry to the ceremonies it made obligatory. The goal seemed to have been to inspire awe and reverence and a sense of holy mystery in the laity, and that it managed to do.

My family were happy parishioners in an old, American-Irish Catholicism, when the church and school and social hall of Holy Angels filled our days with lessons, novenas, rosaries, meetings, choir practice, the major sports, pancake breakfasts, spaghetti dinners, bake sales, dances, and other activities, and it was not unusual to get there for Mass before eight in the morning and leave after eight at night.

We were ever aware, though, that it was the Mass that was central. An old visiting priest once harangued us schoolchildren in his homily: "If you truly believed what is going on here," and he gestured toward the high altar and tabernacle, "you'd be here every day!" And we looked to each other in puzzlement: We *were* there every day; it was the first thing we did before going to the classrooms for religion and the five other, lesser subjects.

The holy nuns who were our teachers taught us to see the

Mass as the occasion where the hunger of our heart would find satisfaction. In fact, it came to seem there was a hole in the day when, on vacation or for some other reason, we did not go to church. I feel that way still.

Jesus taught his disciples to pray, "Give us this day our daily bread," and as the concept of the eucharistic mystery developed over the centuries, the frequency of its celebration increased from weekly assemblies to include the occasional memorials of popular saints, which in turn, through proliferation, led to daily Mass. And through the influence of the religious orders in the Middle Ages, courtly affectations, courtesies, and gestures of homage, such as genuflection, processions, and incensing of the sacrament, gave rise to cultic practices—and, in primitive societies, superstitions—that the Reformation would ridicule and try to halt.

Our church calendar was checkered with them: monthly Benediction, in which the Host was enshrined in a golden monstrance for what was once called "occular communion," and was used to solemnly bless the congregation at the conclusion of a liturgical service; the Forty Hours devotion, in which the Blessed Sacrament was venerated to commemorate the night and day of Christ's Passion; the yearly festival of Corpus Christi, a celebration of eucharistic piety, in which parishioners were urged to increase their active participation in a Latin liturgy they could only follow in the English translation of their *Saint Joseph Missal*. Monsignor Flanagan went still further at Holy Angels by instituting perpetual adoration: The church was open twenty-four hours a day, seven days a week, with one or two parishioners continuously there, praying before Christ in the tabernacle. There were many nights when, on a wander near the neighborhood, and in some state of crisis and desperation, I went inside the near-dark church for a "visit" and saw one or two adorers haloed by the glow of their reading lamps and silently kneeling on prie-dieux near the altar railing, generously giving up an hour of their day to say the rosary or page through their prayer books in a vigil that still strikes me as poignant and chivalrous.

In high school a Jesuit priest encouraged Rob and his classmates to go to weekly Confession, and so he went once, alone. As Rob was saying his prayers afterward, he scanned a church that was otherwise empty and stared at the veiled tabernacle where the Blessed Sacrament was kept, and he remembered the first line of Psalm 84, "How lovely is your dwelling place, O LORD of hosts!" Rob thought, *I have always been happy here,* and it was then he decided he would become a Jesuit.

I have never been so stunned as when he confided that to me. The Jesuit vows of obedience, poverty, and chastity—particularly the latter—seemed hard, onerous, and positively scary to this high school boy. And I was cooling to the Church in my late teens and early twenties, not in the freefall-with-no-parachute way of so many Catholics who call themselves lapsed—I was still a weekly communicant—but oh, what a scoffer I was, a lofty, incredulous, ever-objecting wiseguy slouching in the farthest back pew and just waiting for the priest to screw up. Which he often did in those years when the secrecy and panoply and weird accretions of the Tridentine Rite were giving way to the homely vernacular and folk guitar and roll-your-own liturgies. And the boredom, the abominable boredom. There were priests then—

there regrettably still are—who seemed not to have read a theology book since their ordination, whose interest in their congregations seemed nil, whose homilies were dull, turgid, or haranguing, and who, were they professors offering elective classes in a university setting, would find themselves utterly without students.

I am talking about the sixties and seventies now, when rebellion was à la mode, but my crime was insubordination, not revolution, for I discovered that when I did not go to Mass I missed it. I felt serenity there, even joy; it seemed to make things good and right, and as my attendance at Mass increased in frequency, my sense of the rhythm, history, and logic of the liturgy also grew. Weather, busyness, and the doldrums could still hold me at bay, but for the most part I was hooked. A daily.

Often now, when I find myself in a city of strangers, I find a local Catholic church and go to the first morning or noontime Mass. And in the familiar structure of the eucharistic rites and the faith I presumably share with the assembly, I have a feeling of commonality, of long-lost family, of home.

Even in my childhood, most Catholics did not think it odd that the commemorative meal that the first Christians shared had changed through the ages into an object of adoration and reservation, nor that the simple dining rooms of the first centuries had given way to sanctuaries that resembled the holy of holies where the ark of the covenant was kept. The laity were little more than an afterthought in the rubrics of the *Roman Missal*, and their noninvolvement made it easy to ignore what was going on: It was not uncommon at Mass to see a parishioner strolling around the church lighting votive candles, oblivious to the Consecration even as the shaken bells heralded it. We were called members of Christ's Mystical Body, the Church, but our participation in liturgies was limited to serving the priest, ushering, singing in the choir. We, the unordained, could not touch the consecrated bread, nor the ciborium that contained it. We did not drink the wine. Women could not go beyond the altar railing except for chores like cleaning and lily arranging.

I recall one morning when I was serving the assistant pastor at Communion, holding the gold-plated paten under the chins of those who were receiving so the Host would land on the paten and not the floor should the wafer slip from their tongues. Monsignor Flanagan was helping out by giving Communion farther down the railing, and I heard him roar, "Don't you *dare* touch that!" With shock I turned to see Monsignor in one of his hot-tempered rages, screaming chastisements at a cringing old woman who'd had the gall to try retrieve a fallen Host. *With her hands.*

Rules were rules, after all.

But the Second Vatican Council changed them. In order to re-gain the spirit of the Gospels and the liturgical celebrations of the first Christians, Vatican II urged the conscious and active partici-pation of the laity in the Eucharist. Rescinding the prohibition against vernacular languages in the Roman rite, increasing the number and content of biblical readings, reestablishing old cus-toms such as Communion in the hand and of both kinds, permit-ting the laity to act as deacons, lectors, psalmists, and ministers of the Eucharist, Vatican II sought an *aggiornamento*, a renewal or updating of the institutes and practice of the Church. And it accomplished its goal as no council had since Trent.

I was a lector at Mass for many years before I became a eucharistic minister. I was a college professor, after all, and had read my own fiction in public hundreds of times, so it was not particularly daunting to stand at the lectern, or ambo, and read aloud the Hebrew scriptures, the responsorial psalm, the epistle. Words were familiar and safe. To hand Christ's body and blood to the congregation at Mass, however, seemed such a staggering and godly thing to do that I felt too unworthy to try it.

Then I realized there was an important theological point in that: I am, as we all are, a sinner; but in Christ I am as loved and forgiven as the good thief on the cross; in him my faith and worthiness are sufficient.

And so at noon Mass in the old California mission church of Santa Clara, I have the courage to go up to the tabernacle, genuflect before it just as Monsignor Flanagan would, and get out a ciborium I would not have dared touch in my childhood. And I stand where a railing used to be, holding the consecrated elements of either bread or wine, giving Christ to those holier than me, who walk up with such reverence, simplicity, seriousness, and childlike vulnerability that my eyes sometimes film with tears. It is a gift to me, that giving; it's the glorious feeling I have when I am writing as well as I can, when I feel I am, in ways I have no control of, an instrument of the Holy Being; for I have just an inkling of what Jesus felt when he looked on his friends in mercy and aching love, and I have a sense of why, just before he died, he established this gracious sacrament of himself.

SOURCES

Catechism of the the Catholic Church (New York: Doubleday, 1995).

Johannes H. Emminghaus, *The Eucharist: Essence, Form, Celebration* (Collegeville, MN: Liturgical Press, 1981).

George Fitzgerald, C.S.P., *Handbook of the Mass* (New York: Paulist Press, 1982).

Eugene LaVerdiere, S.S.S., *Dining in the Kingdom of God* (Chicago: Liturgy Training Publications, 1994).

Nathan Mitchell, *Cult and Controversy: The Worship of the Eucharist Outside the Mass* (Collegeville, MN: Liturgical Press, 1990).

Dennis C. Smolarski, S.J., *Eucharistia: A Study of the Eucharistic Prayer* (New York: Paulist Press, 1982).

CONFIRMATION

PAUL MARIANI

Remember: stir into flame the gift of God you received when I placed my hands on you. God gave neither of us a spirit of cowardice. Instead, he gave us a spirit of power, a spirit of love and self-discipline. Do not be ashamed of giving witness to our Lord, nor to me, a prisoner now for his sake. And bear your share of hardship for the Good News with the very strength that comes from God.

—Paul's second letter to Timothy, from Rome, in chains

May 1951. Levittown, Long Island. Beneath the trees, traffic soughs by on Hempstead Turnpike. I stand at the back of St. Bernard's Roman Catholic Church, waiting, along with perhaps thirty other boys and girls, to be confirmed by our bishop. It is a bare, stripped space, more Quaker-like than the neo-Gothic immigrant church, drenched in Carravaggio light and shellac-thick shadows, that was St. John's on New York's 57th and First, where the Queensboro Bridge loomed two blocks north, and just beyond it the small Italian enclave where my father and nine of his brothers and sisters had been born. No, Levittown is another world. Rawer, fresher, offering a new promise. This is an altogether airier, lighter world, the church itself a makeshift affair to accommodate the sudden influx of thousands of new Catholics. It is, in fact, a thinly disguised World War II wooden hangar fleshed out with modest stained glass windows and a small, imitation pre–Vatican II altar up front, flush against the far wall.

Levittown, that uniform, unwieldy Eden built on mud and potato farm and promises, a place with very little history except as farming seasons go, a suburban experiment, an American Mecca to which thousands of New Yorkers, many of them ex-GIs like my father, along with their wives and young families, have journeyed by truck, train, and car to begin a new life for themselves.

A new life. That is what the sisters in their black and white habits adorned with huge rosaries have told us sixth grade confirmandi we are going to receive this very day. Half of all the families in this sprawling collection of Cape Cods and Ranch-style houses are Catholic, another twenty percent Jewish, the rest an amalgam of Protestants. I am eleven years old and—on this particular spring day—with the blue skies peeking in through the windows and doors, I have donned a thin purple polyester robe and been lined up with the others to receive the sacrament of Confirmation, thereby signaling my coming of age in the eyes of the Church.

For two years I have served Mass here, often rising before dawn and riding a ragtag bicycle a mile and a half to assist at the 6:00 A.M. service, or driven here each Sunday in the family's dilapidated Studebaker. Once I tried out for the children's choir, though that experiment ended ingloriously when the tall one-eyed nun with the black eye patch and exquisite ear realized a magpie had come to nest among her nightingales and expelled me from the company of the elect. So be it. But today all of us sixth graders are to be confirmed. My biggest worry is whether, when the bishop strikes me the expected blow across the cheek to remind me that I may someday be called upon to witness with my life for the Faith, I will flinch or not, and it is very important that I prove myself the Lord's true soldier. I have learned my responses from the ubiquitous blue-backed *Baltimore Catechism* and have taken as my confirmation name Saint Christopher, for this is in the years before that worthy saint will be expunged from the canon. Christopher, *Christos feros*, Christ-bearer, his John the Baptist–lookalike image pinned to the visor above the steering wheel to vouchsafe safe passage. Today, with my mother—heavy with her fifth child—and my father and brother and sisters there in the congregation, I proceed slowly down the carpeted main aisle with the other children to be confirmed, to be tapped gently on the cheek by the bishop as I secretly await the descent of the Holy Ghost in the form of fire.

And of course, with the expectation and subsequent disappointment of the ardent millennialist, nothing of the sort happens. I am presented, stammer a word or two to the bishop, receive the oil of anointment, am called by my new name, and return to my pew. And life goes on. There are hugs and handshakes all around, my mother beams, my brother Walter makes a face behind the bishop's resplendent robes. Back at the house there's a small celebration with ice cream and cake. The sun shines, the spring lingers through the long afternoon of fifty years ago.

I look back on that moment, on the innocence of it, and wonder. Years ago the heavenly city of Levittown reached its fiftieth birthday; the prayers we said each Sunday for the conversion of Russia have had their desired effect; the oath we proclaimed once a year at Mass to follow the Church's magisterium on the *Index expurgatorius* and the rulings of the Legion of Decency, the Mc-Carthy period, the deepening chill of the Cold War, the first flush of Vatican II, Vietnam: all of that long ago passed down the windswept corridors of history. At sixteen I entered the Marianist Prep in Beacon, New York, sixty miles north of New York City, to begin preparations for the priesthood amid three or four buildings on an old estate overlooking a mountain (neither Sinai nor Tabor) replete with a modest funicular. I was there to finish my studies—Latin, English, Church history, algebra, civics—before going on to the seminary proper further north at the flint-flaked summit of Mount Marcy in the Adirondacks.

Mostly it is the light I remember now. Light in all seasons: the smoke haze of autumn, the deep cold of January sunshine, the lying awake in the communal dorm listening to thunder roll in over the mountains as if the gods were playing ninepins once again, or listening with hard expectation to the large snow-laden branches of pine trees cracking under the weight of an ice storm, the weird and beautiful peacefulness of it all. But after a year of it, a year that saw the Hungarian Revolution fail as the corpses of the dreaded NKVD piled up and were sprinkled with lime to help them decompose where they'd been executed on the cobblestone streets of Budapest, a year too that saw young Castro preparing to take Havana, I left Beacon to return to my home in Mineola, a dozen miles west of Levittown.

As for the aptly named Beacon, that holy place, where I had grown used to talking to God in the quiet interstices of my days and nights, what of it? Long ago the buildings and the chapel were torn down and the place transformed into a public school. Still, I see it as it was then, nuanced and haloed by its own still light, the place where God took the form of a mountain once, replete with lightning and snow and the ascending tracks running up its spine.

A year later, when I entered college (a Catholic college in the Bronx with the improbable name of Manhattan) I remember once pondering the experience of Pentecost as the Acts of the Apostles tells the story, and thought of the wind roaring through the upper cenacle in the old city of Jerusalem and of the dove descending in fire. I took classes in Church history, ethics, the sacraments, along with English, world history, philosophy, and art. I joined a fraternity and worked nights stacking half-empty shelves in a small A&P in Garden City. Spiritual schizophrenic that I was, I served at Mass in LaSalle Chapel, went to frat parties on Friday nights, and drank. During one spell in my sophomore year I imbibed dangerously until three in the morning, waking at daylight behind the wheel of my battered black Chevy in front of my house in Mineola, vomit congealing on my spiffy green vest. How the hell, I asked myself, had I made it home without killing myself? What was it that had guided me through those thirty miles of the Northern State Parkway in winter darkness to deposit me, against the odds, back home, still in one piece?

At nineteen I met Eileen, the woman who would become my wife. I settled down, studied hard, graduated from Manhattan with a major in English, went on for my master's in the stark snow and ice interior of Hamilton, New York, married my second year there, went on for my doctorate in English at Hunter College, fathered and began to raise three sons, wrote a dissertation on the poetry of Gerard Manley Hopkins, a Victorian Jesuit who left behind a sheaf of napalm-brilliant poems (all unpublished) at the time of his death, having lived and died (at the age of 44) in almost total obscurity.

Then, in early June 1968, the very day Bobby Kennedy died from an assassin's bullet, I received my Ph.D. By then the brushfire war in Vietnam was raging and would continue to rage for another seven years. Declared 4-F because of my hearing, I instead took a job teaching twentieth-century poetry at UMass, Amherst, and settled in for the long haul. Teaching at a public university taught me early on to check my ardor for things religious at the threshold to the classroom. Less often now I thought about the dark dove descending with its ability to transform. A metaphor like everything else, I began thinking. Pentecost as pure poetry. The kind of thing necessary perhaps to the initiatory stages of Christianity, the age of the apostles, the age of the martyrs. But not operative, surely, at the close of the second Christian millenium.

Besides, if the truth be told, one sensed—especially among one's academic peers—a sort of quiescent, genteel, and occasionally confrontational form of anti-Catholicism. Many of my colleagues considered themselves former Catholics or, worse, "recovering" Catholics. None in my department (which was then one hundred strong) except myself were Catholics, or at least "practicing" Catholics, as the tired jargon went. Once I listened as an older colleague—a man in his fifties with a national reputation—talked of the wafer god Catholics believed in. It was as if I had become invisible to him, even though I was standing next to him. Weirdly, the comment had not been uttered with animosity, but merely as if that were the way things must seem to any straight-thinking Ph.D. this far along in the post-Christian twentieth century.

Divorces were prevalent, free love the new drug of choice. In the first two years after my arrival at the university, many of my married colleagues, especially the younger ones, divorced or separated, some scattering children in their wake. Some—it was a new phenomenon for someone from the provinces like myself actually to observe—took up with partners of the same sex. Drugs, especially marijuana and LSD, were everywhere, among faculty and students alike. I saw—as Allen Ginsberg had said a dozen years before—the best minds of my generation destroyed, including eighteen- and nineteen-year-olds carried off to hospitals in the middle of the night, screaming and suffering from monstrous hallucinations. Something was descending. Not the dove, not Pentecostal fire, but napalm on rice paddies and jungle hideouts in Vietnam, and then, like some dark karma, in the form of roiling fires on Detroit, Harlem, Watts.

Through it all Eileen and I continued to take our three small sons to Sunday Mass at St. Mary's in nearby Turners Falls, a small nineteenth-century model industrial town that like so many

New England towns, had years before begun its slow smoking decay, following an early, short-lived phoenix burst of promise. The town had been built rapidly in the 1880s, as the brick buildings along Avenue A still attest, the population consisting then of French Canadians who had settled here in search of better jobs and a warmer climate. There were also the Poles and Irish who had come to work the farms and the wood pulp factories along the Connecticut River. In the late 1960s their descendants still clung to the town proudly and fiercely. It was here, among working-class people very much like my own parents, that I had decided to settle.

Thirty years ago Turners and environs were very quiet. Little ever seemed to happen here to warrant front-page news, and people liked it that way. Then, one day early in 1972, our small community was stunned by the news of a double murder. The owner of an auto shop in Greenfield, the larger town just across the river, had been brutally murdered by members of a group calling themselves the Troy Gang. It was a revenge killing, it turned out, a way for one of the gang to get back at the owner for firing him. The second victim, a man like myself in his early thirties with a young family, was Ed Flavin, an accountant, someone I knew from church, who just happened to be in the shop the night the Troy Gang decided to make its move. No matter that Ed was in the shop working on the books. He was there, and so would have to be disposed of as well. He was bound, gagged with duct tape, forced to watch the owner's throat slit and then see him bludgeoned to death with a ballpeen hammer, before Ed himself was given a bullet to the back of the head in classic executioner's style.

Two days before Ed was killed I had passed him in the basement hall of St. Mary's as he came out of his sixth grade Confraternity of Christian Doctrine (CCD) class. We exchanged a simple greeting as I walked by to pick up my kids from Sunday school. Even now, after twenty-seven years, that moment of passing remains vivid. I can see his shy brown eyes swimming behind his glasses in the reflected light, his serious demeanor broken by a slight, quizzical smile, one of his own children clinging to him. So very much alive, a man with two jobs trying to make ends meet, teaching Sunday school, and now gone in an unreal instant. A week after his death, I found myself—driven by an inner prompting that would not let me rest—going to the pastor and volunteering to take over Ed's religion class. It was a small gesture, but it was something, and my own sons were already being taught by other volunteers. It was time to step in and do something. An absence, a violent absence, had been effected, and I knew someone would have to fill it. Why not myself?

And so began fifteen years of teaching Sunday school—a clump of years, a lacuna, another clump—sixth, then seventh, then eighth, and up to the eleventh grade, the Confirmation class. These were classes of fifteen to eighteen students, mostly kids from the local high school, with a few coming over from the surrounding private schools: Stoneleigh-Burnham, Northfield-Mount Hermon, Deerfield Academy. Good kids, all of them, some of them faithful, intelligent, from good families, loving families, kids who could be found at Sunday Masses, often with their parents and siblings, people it was a pleasure to speak with for a moment or two on the way out of church. Some of these kids you didn't see again for years, and then there they would be, a baby in the young mother's arms, the young father holding the hand of a toddler, winking and smiling, as if to say, "Bet you never thought you'd see *me* here again, didja?"

It was a standing joke between the parish priest, Father Aksamit, and myself that Confirmation might better be called the Sacrament of Departure. Departure from religious instruction, a swan song to the Church itself. At the beginning of each May, the bishop would come up from Springfield to confer the sacrament, the kids would dress up, the young women in dresses, the young men in white shirts and ties. Spruced-up young adults, proud to be there with their sponsors and families. Individually, in the setting of the Mass, each would be called up before the bishop, give his or her name—the name they themselves had chosen (Saints Wendy and Cliff were out, I had to explain)—and the bishop would anoint them with the seal of the Holy Spirit.

Afterward, there would be coffee and cake, pictures with the bishop, a few pleasantries exchanged, and then the confirmandi, the future hope of the community, were out the door. Too frequently it was the last time I ever saw them. After a year of preparation, after long discussions about their role in the Church, about what it meant to be receiving the sacrament of Confirmation, the intense discussions about the dangerous and wonderful waters they would soon be crossing, they were simply gone. Many parents, it turned out, had actually made contracts with their kids. Attend the monthly three-hour sessions, don't cause any trouble, get the sacrament, and then they would lay off them. If the kids didn't want to go to church anymore, so be it. They were tired of trying to force them. And besides, many of the parents themselves had long since ceased going to church.

I was used to lecturing students at the university, and studiously avoiding their private lives, except when someone was obviously in trouble (when I did—discreetly—what little I could), and so I was used to results. Papers turned in, graded, revised, regraded. A good teacher, so my evaluations read. Knows his shit. Tough but fair. But Confirmation class. *That* I counted as an experiment that was at best a qualified success.

"That's the trouble, Paul," Father Aksamit reminded me one evening as we closed up the basement hall where I taught my Confirmation class. "You want to think of this as a year-long course, with some exam at the end. But the Holy Spirit works on a different timetable. Many of these kids will be back. Maybe not for years. Maybe not here. But the Spirit will be working in them in its own good time." "One sows," Jesus reminded his disciples. "Another reaps."

Besides, Father Aksamit had had the benefit of having heard the confessions of some of these kids, and so knew better than I what they were up against and where their hearts were, and he told me he'd often been heartened by what he'd learned in the confessional. Besides, there was my own youthful life to think back on and wince over. At the beginning of his own ministry, concerned for his own flock, Father Hopkins had put it down in a poem. The truth, he realized, was that we never really got the whole picture on anyone else. We got glimpses, even perhaps an occasional insight, but the rest was mist and darkness. Only the Lord continued to follow, long after the rest of us had gone on to other concerns. "Death or distance soon consumes them," Hopkins had written:

Wind

What most I may eye after, be in at the end
I cannot, and out of sight is out of mind.

Christ minds: Christ's interest, what to avow or amend
There, éyes them, heart wánts, care haúnts, foot fóllows kínd,
Their ránsom, théir rescue, ánd first, fást, last friénd.

A sacrament in search of a theology. That is how one Jesuit theologian has half-jokingly described Confirmation. Over the course of the past two thousand years, the origins of the sacrament of Confirmation have been questioned, debated, defined and redefined, affirmed and denied by various groups within the community who broadly call themselves Christians. For most Protestant denominations Confirmation is not even recognized as a valid sacrament. After all, these Christians argue, Jesus himself never confirmed anyone, and the rite of Confirmation lacks the clear, stark outlines of either Baptism or the Eucharist. At best, according to this line of reasoning, Confirmation was initiated not by Christ but by the apostles, or even later, and so has no validity except as a Church ritual. And so, in their fervor to rid the Church of all excrescencies and return it to its original purity, many Protestants did away with Confirmation.

Unlike Baptism and Eucharist—the bedrock sacraments—Christ never spoke of Confirmation as such. But then he never used the defining word, "Christians," either. For Catholics, there is, besides the scriptures, a rich mother lode of tradition for guidance. But even in the New and Old Testaments there are a number of passages attesting to the ancient significance and force of the twin gestures of the laying on of hands and the anointing of kings and priests.

The Catholic church, both in her Eastern and Western rites, points to the following biblical passages, among others, in support of Confirmation. In Luke's gospel, committed to paper sometime between A.D. 70 and 80, Jesus speaks of the Holy Spirit as the Advocate, the Comforter, the One who is to come after him, that is, after he himself would be raised from the dead and glorified. For its first hearers, undergoing persecution by both the Jewish authorities—themselves under siege—as well as the Roman authorities who had come to distrust the new sect of Christians—Jesus' reminder that the Holy Spirit would be with them when they were dragged into the courts or the synagogues had to have sustained them in a time of terrible stress. "Do not worry about how to defend yourselves or what to say"—the words of Jesus, who had himself been forcibly dragged before the Sanhedrin and before Pilate—"because when the time comes, the Holy Spirit will teach you what you must say."

And then there is John, recalling some six decades after the event Jesus' last will and testament spoken in the upper room the night before his death, promising his followers that he would not leave them orphans, but would send the Paraclete, the Spirit, when he himself was gone. "Unless I go," he had told them, "the Advocate will not come to you. But if I do go, I will send him to you." His work as a man was nearing its conclusion; he had done all he could, and *as a man*, his career had been capped by seemingly total failure. Most, uncomprehending, had turned away, and only a remnant had remained faithful. And in a few hours even those would scatter at the first breath of murderous resistance, including the man Jesus had nicknamed the Rock. They would crumble from within, betrayed by one of their own. But it would all be necessary, the whole illogical, nightmarish scenario, if Jesus was to win out over his real enemies, sin and fear and death. He would first have to empty himself on the cross—a complete abandonment, an emptying that would leave him a worm, his great heart shattered by a soldier's javelin—if he was ever to be lifted and glorified by the Father. It would have to be a free and total gift of himself as a man accepted by man's Creator, in that lifting up onto the cross lifting every one of us with him to another necessary, impossible dimension. Then, and only then, in the release of Jesus' blood and spirit, would the Spirit—Christ's Spirit and the Father's Spirit—flood the world with His grace.

The operative passage most often cited for the Catholic rite of Confirmation occurs in Acts 8:14–17, but the passage must first be properly framed and understood. If the original band of disciples thought the work of redemption and salvation was over with Jesus' death and resurrection, they were soon disabused of that fairy-tale ending, just as Jesus had had to disabuse them of the idea that a political settlement (ousting the Romans from Judea) could ever be the answer to their problems. The problems went far deeper than that, Jesus had had to show them, and included a radical fracture with God and therefore with their own psyches. The work—the real work, in fact—was just beginning. Like a good line officer, Jesus had led the way, had given the example, an example he wanted his followers now to begin to put into practice.

Nor would he leave them to their own ineffectual devices, for he knew too well human weakness, knew the very men he had set aside to do his work would scatter like scared sheep when, at the darkest hour, the wolf should enter the fold. And so he had prayed for them, especially Peter, poor blustering Peter, that Satan would not crush him. No, Jesus would send them another, the Spirit, the Comforter, to steady them, even in the face of the unspeakable. We had smashed the garden, and like a good Father, he would give us the responsibility and the wherewithal to put the garden back into some semblance of order. It would be our way of participating in the great work of restoring God's first kingdom.

In one of his last post-Resurrection appearances, Jesus had told his disciples to go out from Jerusalem into the surrounding countryside to preach the good news of salvation, beginning with Judea and Samaria and moving on to Rome and the ends of the world. Judea was one thing—for these were Jews who followed the Way of Christ as they spoke and prayed with their fellow Jews in the Temple and in the synagogues.

But Samaria? That was another story. That would be rather like Jews proselytizing the West Bank Palestinians today. The hatreds and mutual distrusts between Jews and Samaritans had been there centuries before Jesus had come on the scene, and they would continue for centuries to come. Persecution and unrest in

Judea and in Jerusalem—beginning with the stoning of Stephen and moving out from there, with Saul of Tarsus (later Saint Paul) taking a leading role in the persecutions and arrests of those errant brothers who were following the Way of Jesus. And so the disciples had moved out into less hostile territory, including Samaria, where Saul and his zealous followers would not be welcome. And soon Philip was preaching and effecting cures there, with the result that a number of Samaritans began coming over to the new religion.

Then word came back to the apostles in Jerusalem that Samaritans were being baptized, though "only in the name of the Lord." It is clear from this passage that the church leadership from the very beginning did not take Baptism as sufficient for full initiation into the Christian community, and so they sent Peter and John, two of the church's leaders, to go and pray over the Samaritans that they might also "receive the Holy Spirit," as they themselves had received it on that first Pentecost. Like Jesus they had been baptized, surely in the Jordan River at the hands of John the Baptist. But though they had entered into a special covenant with God in that act, the baptism had primarily been a cleansing, a washing away of sin, a preparatory gesture only, however necessary. It had been in a sense a clearing of the field. The Gospels speak of the Holy Spirit descending on Jesus after his Baptism, and of the Father's voice calling Jesus his beloved son, the anointed one, the king, much as Samuel had been sent to anoint Jesus' ancestor, the great David, as king of the Jewish nation a thousand years before.

In the three years during which they had followed Jesus, the disciples had learned—from misconstruing again and again what Jesus had told them—that something more, something crucial, beyond Baptism would be needed if they were to carry out the Lord's work. What would be needed in addition would be the descent of the Holy Spirit over them. Indeed, the same Spirit who would give them knowledge and wisdom and understanding and courage would give them discernment and right judgment and a spirit of reverence. And he would give them something more: a sense of awe, of holy wonder at the workings of the Lord in their lives.

In short, Jesus promised his followers his own Spirit, his own life. Jesus had pointed to the Paraclete as coming only when he himself was gone—after his death, after his Father had glorified him by raising his beaten body from the dead, after his appearances to the disciples at Emmaus and Jerusalem and along the Sea of Galilee, after his ascension. And so, on that first Pentecost morning, at nine o'clock—fifty days after the Passover and the Resurrection—the disciples, Jesus' mother among them, having gathered in the upper room to wait with patience and prayer, were suddenly shaken by the sound of a strong wind whirling through the room, followed by what appeared to be tongues of fire settling over them.

A reversal of the curse of the Tower of Babel, I remember thinking, the curse of misunderstanding, confusion, and isolation wrought by hubris, a reversal effected by total obedience, a radical emptying of the self, uniting the disciples' words to the Word, so that language reversed itself to become not a barrier now but a bridge. Now, as the disciples spoke in their northcountry

Galilean accents, each was understood by the crowds outside, made up of fellow Jews whose ancestors had been scattered by the various Diasporas, and who had come now to the holy city of Jerusalem. Parthians these were, and Medes and Elamites, citizens from the region of Mesopotamia (the ancient land between the rivers). People from "Judea and Cappadocia, Pontus and Asia, Phrygia and Pamphylia, Egypt and the parts of Libya around Cyrene; as well as visitors from Rome—Jews and converts to Judaism alike—Cretans and Arabs," each hearing in their own language *about the marvels of God.*

A sign of unity, then, a sign of communion, this instant translation for the plethora of nationals assembled there for Pentecost, the harvest feast. And what a harvest it was. Pentecost: the Church's birthday, when the Spirit turned these timid followers into preachers harvesting souls, three thousand that very day alone.

Consider Peter, waffling and fumbling at least as often as he hit the mark, Jesus praising him because he'd been bold enough to recognize Jesus as the Messiah, the Christ, the anointed of God. It is the same Peter who would try to rewrite the script of salvation by insisting that he had a better plan than the one of which Jesus had spoken: of going up to Jerusalem, of being turned over to the religious leaders to be flogged and crucified. No wonder Jesus had cut Peter short, calling him Satan, ordering him to get behind him. Peter, poor Peter, insisting as I would have that he would never abandon his savior, then in rapid succession, like three shots, denying him three times.

"Do you love me, Peter?" the risen Christ had asked him, using the verb *agape*, the highest form of love. Yes, Peter assured him, and if not with the highest love, then surely he loved him like a brother (*philo*). Then feed my lambs, Christ had told him. Then a second time, Jesus asking him, and again Peter answering that he loved him like a brother. And again Jesus telling him, it would be enough, if Peter would only take care of his flock. Then a third time, Jesus lowering the stakes, "Peter, do you love me as a brother?' As a brother, Lord. Then, Peter, remember to feed my sheep. But of course Jesus knew his man, for in time—thirty years of it—Peter would learn enough about divine love to follow his master right into the jaws of death, embracing the very crucifixion he had turned from in fear.

But now, at this first Pentecost, touched by the fire of the Spirit, the same Peter who had fled from the Temple precincts as they led his master away is suddenly a changed man: confident, assured, fully willing to assume the leadership to which Jesus had called him. "Make no mistake about it, but listen to what I have to say," Peter tells the assembled crowds in the heart of the holy city. "I will make you fishers of men," Jesus had told Peter and the others, using a metaphor these fishermen would have understood. And to bring home his point, he had had Peter cast his empty net over the side of his boat. And suddenly Peter, discouraged from having caught nothing all through the long night, is hauling in enough fish to nearly break the net. And again now, on this first Pentecost morning, hauling in three thousand souls as a first down payment on a glorious future.

How often I have wished my handful of charges might somehow witness to the presence of the Spirit, to feel God working sensibly in their lives as I have felt him. Mostly, though, it did not happen, or more precisely, did not happen in any way that I could see while they were in my charge. This should have come as no surprise, really, for experience has taught me that the Spirit descends upon us not when we expect, but when we are ready to receive him. I have seen the young moved by the experience of Teen Encounter, my own three sons among them, but more often than not this was an emotional response, sometimes verging on a kind of mild (and *benign*) hysteria, though sometimes real change began even that early. And once, at a Mass for my class, in which Father Darcy, the motorcycle-riding, drum-playing young priest, was taking us step by step through the Mass, I saw the biggest guy in the group, a quiet, powerful linebacker on the local team, fall suddenly to his knees with a thud at the consecration, and everyone, including myself, followed suit. Who, after all, can measure such things? Did not Jesus tell us that the Spirit moved as the Spirit willed, unpredictable as the wind itself?

Sometimes I think of my own journey, who studied for the priesthood at seventeen, and then left, though God knows something obviously took hold then, despite my own repeated failures, and never let me go. For me, the dove's most sensible descent occurred when I was thirty-two, married, the father of three small sons, and it happened in the basement of a yellow-brick Catholic school in Holyoke, Massachusetts. Two women from St. Mary's had stopped me in the doorway on my way to teach Sunday school and had asked if I'd like to make a Cursillo. I'd never even heard the word before, but thinking it was a retreat of some kind and something I knew I needed, I said yes.

Fifty men in a basement on Memorial Day weekend, 1972, beautiful weather, three days of talks by men, not one of whom I'd ever met before. The retreat began traditionally enough that first evening. There were the Stations of the Cross, a homily by a priest, confessions, silence, followed by a miserable night on an army cot in a nondescript classroom shared with fifteen other men, shades drawn for privacy, someone snoring heavily next to me. Saturday morning, more of the same: a few talks by laymen and a priest, breaks for coffee and a few jokes.

But after lunch, the talks suddenly became more interesting. Men began sharing their most intimate secrets, their failings, their God longings. A man, an ex-paratrooper, had lost his little boy years before and broke down with the memory of it, reminding me that I had three little boys at home. A psychologist spoke of his time in the air force as a SAC bomber pilot. When it finally dawned on him that the nuclear bomb he was carrying was capable of annihilating, he refused to fly another mission, a decision that cost him his career. Another spoke of the destruction his alcoholism had wrought in his family, and how he had finally turned to God when he knew he could no longer help himself. Another, a big burly man who loved sports, spoke of how he had finally come to love his severely retarded son.

At some point I began weeping, cursing myself for my weakness before these other men, abruptly pushing back my chair and leaving the room. A priest who was also a family counselor got up to try and comfort me, but I pushed him away and climbed the basement steps three at a time to get out of there. This wasn't how a goddamn retreat was supposed to go, I kept saying to myself, feeling I'd been coldcocked. Upstairs, sitting by my cot, gasping for air and trying to understand why I had been so violently affected, I felt as if I had been touched, as if somehow I could finally begin to love my bastard self and begin to love others in return.

Father Hopkins speaks repeatedly of his fears of saying yes and yes again, when somewhere beneath it all he fears he is still saying no. On Memorial Day, 1972, I finally understood that I had been holding back, with one qualified yes after another, and that something in my battered dogbrain had finally let go and said yes. Yes to life, yes to God. A turning point had been reached.

When at last I went back downstairs I found the men gathered about their tables, discussing the talk and drawing makeshift stick figures on posters, replete with sayings like, "Bloom where you're planted" and "God loves you," generalities to hide deeper truths for which the language was missing. Some were standing over at a table drinking coffee, some in concentrated conversation. I returned to my table and listened. But already everything was different. I would change; I would reach out in ways I hadn't before; I would love my family; I would try to live more honestly and with greater courage.

This was not for thought, though of course thought would enter it. No, this went deeper than thought, filling the deepest abysses of the self. This was a reprieve, a new life. Suddenly John and Luke and Matthew and Mark and Paul flamed into life, and I felt more connected to them than I did to the events history had thrown up at me: Vietnam, civil rights, affirmative action, even my life at the university. In that afternoon, that otherwise nonde-script afternoon, with traffic soughing by on Route 10, the Spirit had conspired to dissolve time itself, and what the disciples had experienced on that first Pentecost I too was tasting just now.

By the time the third evening of the retreat weekend had arrived, I stood before a gathering of several hundred women and men and told them that, though I did not yet know them all personally, I knew I loved them. The truth is—and I speak this from witness—that from where I stood, they all seemed washed in a golden light, ordinary folks from Chicopee and Springfield and Holyoke, from Greenfield and North Adams, from Indian Orchard and Brimfield and Palmer, aglow with an inner light. I rubbed my eyes and looked again, but the light remained.

In the intervening quarter century, I have tried to show them and others I have met along the way that what I feel for them really is love. Slowly, steadily, in ways I cannot easily measure, so subtle are the workings of the Spirit, I have tried to fulfill what began that night. I became a joiner; I did what I was asked and more, every yes being amply repaid, every no leaving a lingering sadness. In time I became a lector and a Eucharistic minister, distributing communion to the faithful, and for years to the elderly at the local nursing home. I continued to teach CCD, to serve on committees—some so boring and long I had to hide my yawns and muffle my screams. At the university I tried to teach as if it were a calling, as in fact it is. Amid backslidings and crumplings—some of them serious, at least one nearly lethal to the well-being of my family—I have sought daily to grow in the Spirit.

So, knowing all this, knowing how the Spirit had had patiently to wait for me to turn, how could I really expect my seventeen-year-old charges to respond to what I was trying to tell them? It is a gift, after all, that the Spirit offers, and not some sort of calculus, and all I can do along with others who labor in the field is prepare the soil. Too much has yet to be experienced by the young, who, like the youthful Saint Augustine, and like myself, have been heard to say, "Lord, change me and make me thine ... but not yet."

Part of the problem, of course, is what we demand of Confirmation, and, by extension, what we demand of God. Consider for a moment the kinds of debates that have swirled about the meaning of this sacrament. From that first Pentecost, the Church knew something radical had occurred, that the spreading of the Good News would be met with serious opposition, lethal opposition in fact. That the Church would find opposition all along the way, just as their Teacher had—opposition not only from without but from within—and that the unity among his followers that Jesus had so fervently prayed for would be tested and frayed. That brother and sister would argue and fight as both read the message of Christ by their own lights. The Spirit of truth and discernment would be needed every step of the way, and that would mean prayer and wisdom and knowledge and courage, an abiding sense that the issues raised really were a matter of life and death.

But what, after all, was Confirmation? The descent of the Holy Spirit upon Christ's followers, a completion of Baptism, a steadying and a strengthening, a conferral of the gifts that would allow one to meet the challenges of an uncomprehending world with knowledge and wisdom and forbearance and courage, much as Abraham and Isaac and Moses and Elijah and countless others had borne witness centuries before.

When Jesus, filled with the Holy Spirit, as Luke tells us, began his public ministry following his forty-day trial in the wilderness, he went back to his hometown and there, on the Sabbath, preached in the local synagogue. Opening the scroll of Isaiah, he found the passage he was looking for, and then told the assembly that the Jesus they were looking at now was not the same Jesus who had grown up alongside them. Summoned by His father and by the Spirit, he had been changed, and now he was beginning his public ministry by bringing his townspeople the first fruits of the Good News: "The Spirit of the Lord has been given me, for he has anointed me. He has sent me to bring the good news to the poor, to proclaim liberty to captives, and to the blind new sight, to set the downtrodden free, to proclaim the Lord's year of favor." Then he told the assembly that the passage he had just read them was being fulfilled even as they listened.

And so it would be with his followers. They too, he promised, would be given the same Holy Spirit he had been given. But how was the gift of the Spirit to be administered to others?

The Catholic church teaches that there are seven sacraments. Three of these—Baptism, Confirmation, and Eucharist—are sacraments of initiation, and were for a long time conferred on the catechumen, the initiate, in the space of a single evening, the holiest night of the Christian year, the Easter Vigil. These three sacraments are in fact still conferred one after the other where there are adult converts to the faith. It can be an awesome experience, witnessing the conferral of these sacraments.

Confirmation is bestowed with two gestures, ancient in themselves. First, the laying on of hands, usually on the head of the one receiving the gift, signifying the transmission of power, a gesture Paul himself used in conferring the sacrament. This was the earliest gesture. Very early on it began to be accompanied by a second: the anointing with chrism (olive oil mixed with aromatic balsam), a mixture used in the anointing of kings and priests. *Chrism,* the same word that gives us the name for the Christ—the anointed one, the Messiah, the Chosen—and from which our own identities as Christians derives. Only much later, during the Middle Ages, was the ritual slap on the cheek added: a remnant of a time when knights, bowing before their lords, were struck on the shoulder with the flat of a sword blade to remind them of the mortal combat that awaited them somewhere down the line. A knightly gesture, for all its symbolic power, quietly dropped when Vatican II returned to even more ancient rituals.

The exact words spoken over the confirmed by the apostles are themselves a matter of conjecture. No doubt the original words of the apostles when they came to Samaria to anoint the new converts were short and to the point. "Receive the Holy Spirit." "Be sealed in the Holy Spirit." That seems to have been the gist of what was spoken with the laying on of hands.

In time the words were codified so that today the bishop or his representative extends his hands over those about to be confirmed, first reminding them of the intimate connection between

Baptism and Confirmation, before asking the Holy Spirit to bestow on those to be confirmed His sevenfold graces:

> All powerful God, Father of our Lord Jesus Christ,
> by water and the Holy Spirit
> you freed your sons and daughters from sin
> and gave them new life.
> Send your Holy Spirit upon them
> to be their helper and guide.
> Give them the spirit of wisdom and understanding,
> the spirit of right judgment and courage,
> the spirit of knowledge and reverence.
> Fill them with the spirit of wonder and awe in your presence.
> We ask this through Christ our Lord.

As with each of the sacraments, the heart of the message is always very simple: *Send forth your Spirit on these.* Everything else is an embellishment—like the cup that in time became the silver chalice—of the great simplicity of God's freely bestowed gifts.

Three sacraments, then, originally administered as parts of a single rite initiating the catechumen into the mysteries of Christ's life. But as the Church grew, changes necessarily occurred. Early on it was only adults who were deemed ready to enter the Church, and then only after lengthy preparation. Normally the local bishop presided at these rituals. But then the Church began racing like fire through dry brush, not in spite of persecutions, but because of them. Bishops could not be everywhere, and so some of their authority had to be delegated to other priests. In time too there was a call among Christian families to see their children enter the Church as early as possible. Infant Baptisms became the norm, and these were administered by local priests and deacons, as well as by others in times of emergency. Eucharist could also be offered to the baptized. But confirmations were still clustered and administered by the bishop whenever he was able to visit these remote areas. This might be once a year, sometimes only once every five or ten years. (Indeed, in the seventeenth century in Ireland under the English, or in the Spanish, French, and especially the English colonies of the New World, many who were baptized went to their graves without ever once seeing a bishop and being confirmed.)

There were other changes; for instance, in the name of the sacrament. In the Eastern churches, the sacrament is called Chrismation—an anointing with chrism, or *myron* (Greek for "perfume"), the name emphasizing the anointing of the individual, and it is the priest rather than the bishop who administers it, though the chrism is blessed by the bishop beforehand. In the West, the sacrament came to be called Confirmation, a word that carries with it something of the Roman administrative language which came in with the Edict of Constantine and the privileging of Christianity as the official state religion in the fourth century. It is a word that suggests a *ratification* and a *strengthening* of the gifts of Baptism, confirming what was begun with Baptism. For centuries now sponsors have stood in for the infant to make the promises that at Confirmation the individual would be asked to make in his or her own name. So with me, in a ritual I have no way of recalling, with my Aunt Katherine and my Uncle Louis standing in for me in the early spring of 1940, in the Church of the Precious Blood in Astoria, Queens.

It is only with Tertullian in the fourth century that the three acts of initiation, Baptism, Confirmation, and Eucharist, were clearly distinguished. "After being immersed," Tertullian explains, "we are thoroughly anointed with a blessed unction according to the ancient rule." This oil, he says, "runs down our bodies"— rather like athletes preparing for the games—"but affects us spiritually." Then there was the laying on of hands, in which the celebrant called upon the Holy Spirit to descend on the catechumen. The body, Tertullian explains, was first washed in Baptism to cleanse the spirit of sin. Then it was anointed that the spirit might be consecrated and illuminated. Finally, the catechumen was given the Eucharist that the spirit might be nourished.

As the Scholastics of the thirteenth and fourteenth century attempted to catalogue and define practices that had been evolving over the centuries, they attempted to probe the deeper nature of sacramentality, defining just how Baptism differed from Confirmation. Lanfranc, Anselm, Abelard, Hugh of St. Victor, Peter Lombard, Albertus Magnus, Thomas Aquinas, Alexander of Hales, Bonaventure, Duns Scotus: All attempted to shed light on the workings of the Spirit.

Eventually issues arose as to the very sacramentality of Confirmation. The Franciscans taught that the Holy Ghost had instituted it, acting either directly through the apostles or through the Church. Alexander of Hales, in fact, thought Confirmation was established only in the ninth century with the Council of Meaux, though prepared for as a rite from apostolic times. But Thomas

Aquinas differed. Only Christ could have instituted the sacrament, he argued. True, Christ had not shown or performed (*exhibendo*) the sacrament himself, but he had promised it when he had said, as the evangelist John reports (16:7), "If I do not go, the Paraclete will not come to you; but if I go, I will send Him to you."

Thomas clinched his argument by adding that the fullness of the Holy Spirit could not in the nature of things be given before Christ's resurrection and ascension, as John himself had also explained (7:39): "As yet the Spirit was not given, because Jesus had not yet been glorified." With modifications, Thomas's formulation would be the one upheld by the Council of Trent, amid the wracking turmoil of the Protestant Reformation.

Whom was the sacrament for? And when was it to be administered? The first question is easier to answer. Every baptized person, the Church teaches, is to receive the sacrament *at the appropriate time*. And when was that? Over the centuries Baptism was shifted backwards in time to a child's infancy, the sooner, the popular reasoning went, to make sure the child was under the Church's protection. Similarly, the initial reception of the Eucharist was pushed back, especially with the urging of Pius X early in the twentieth century. Seven became the age at which most Catholics received their First Communion.

But Confirmation created a more vexing problem. In the early church, the sequence had been Baptism, followed by Confirmation, followed by the reception of the Eucharist. In time, however, Eucharist came to follow Baptism, though it was still not uncommon for some children to be confirmed at seven or eight, prior to their initial reception of the Eucharist. Early on the Church settled on "the age of discretion" as the time at which Catholics were to receive Confirmation, though in extraordinary situations, such as danger of death, even the very young might be confirmed.

But what was "the age of discretion"? Certainly some matured more quickly than others. Nor was adult faith synonymous with physical maturity. After all, in the long history of the Church, children had often been called upon to witness to the faith and— as Saint Thomas had phrased it—"through the strength of the Holy Spirit have bravely fought for Christ even to the shedding of their blood." I myself received Confirmation at the age of eleven, when I knew painfully little. My own sons received the sacrament at the age of sixteen or seventeen. Older and surely wiser than I had been, and perhaps by then they had reached the age of discretion—except when it came to driving.

So Confirmation came to be associated in the popular mind with the rite of passage to adulthood, not unlike the Jewish rite of Bar Mitzvah, though (alas) certainly Confirmation usually commands a far less rigorous Scripture orientation, try as some may to make preparation for Confirmation more intellectually demanding. Still, the gift of the Spirit, I have had to remind myself, is a gift open to all, an unmerited election that needs no one's ratification to become effective, since the Spirit moves as the Spirit will. All the Confirmation teacher can do is try to lead the young toward a better understanding of Christ and a greater familiarity with the Holy Spirit. It is the Spirit who works in us as he will, prompting and leading us, even—as Father Hopkins wrote in a beautiful, homespun metaphor—cheering us on as we come down the home stretch. After all, what we as teachers are doing is preparing the next generation to take up the torch as we pass it on. For they too must one day assume responsibility for the Faith, as that Faith has been passed on from generation to generation in an unbroken succession since the time of Mary, Peter, John, James, and Paul.

Which makes it all the sadder, if the truth be told, to see the young heading for the exits of the church as soon as they have received their sacrament of departure. I gather with a number of Catholic men roughly my own age. Teachers, some of us, bankers, architects, psychologists, a dealer in rare paper, a printer, a construction worker who operates heavy equipment, a trucker, a parish priest. Over the years we have spent untold hours sharing our concerns about the young, about where they are going, about what they will do, about the future of their faith. Recently the high school massacre at Littleton, Colorado, has been very much on our minds, and we have asked ourselves if what happened there could happen here, among our own children.

Yes, we think, though we pray it will not. And then suddenly, electrically, the mind darts back to what the heart yearns to hear. The story—assigned in the subsequent confusion, perhaps, to one young woman rather than another—of a girl, in the electric horror of imminent death, already shot by her deranged classmate standing in a black trench coat over her while he reloaded his TEC 9 semiautomatic, taunting her with the question if she believed in God now. She could see others besides herself had been shot, had heard the sharp metallic reports of gunfire in the hallway, then seen a student rushing terrified into the library where she and dozens of others cowered under chairs and study tables, then the killers entering, then more shots as her classmates crumpled.

A young woman saying yes, and when asked why, answering simply that her parents had raised her to believe. Or in the other version, a simple yes. But either way a yes. It is the one question, finally, as Hopkins says, we all must answer with our lives one way or the other. And so, with the business end of a gun staring her in the face, she considered for a moment, and thought of the consequences of witnessing to what she knew to be the truth, and managed, I must believe, with the strength of the same Holy Spirit who has touched me and so many others, to utter, as I too should want to utter, the one word neccessary as the dark dove descended: her world-resounding, God-affirming Yes.

Pentecost, 1999

SOURCES

Catechism of the Catholic Church (New York: Doubleday, 1995).
The Catholic Encyclopedia (New York: Robert Appleton, 1914).
Gerard Manley Hopkins, "The Lantern Out of Doors," from *The Poetical Works of Gerard Manley Hopkins*, edited by Norman H. Mackenzie (Oxford: Clarendon, 1990).

Matrimony

PAULA HUSTON

We are sunk deep in a slow river of people, pilgrims pushed so close together we can smell each other's sweat, and we have been in this line for over an hour. Pigeons, some of them with their toes singed off by the burning cobblestones, peck around our feet, murmuring in pigeon glossolalia; the industrially polluted waters that surround this sinking medieval city wink oily rainbows at the sun. A few feet ahead of us is the cathedral of San Marco, where the pilgrim river is forcing its way uphill and through a narrow gate, a metal police barricade guarded by two handsome young Venetians in black slacks and gray bowling shirts. Their dark eyes flash busily over us, passing quick but irrevocable judgment; when one of them holds up his blue sign, the river stops, swirls, and somebody steps out of it, turned away at the last moment at the very doors of the church.

"What do they think they're doing?" mutters a red-faced Brit with a Minolta around his neck. "Separating out the sheep from the goats?" There is nervous laughter in our section of the line, quickly quelled. We have been standing in the sun too long to risk the wrath of the gatekeepers.

The blue signs stop and start us; I look up and up, craning my neck to see the great domes of the Byzantine cathedral lifting above us into the hot sky, while behind me, my family shuffles and sighs. As usual, they are here under duress; I am the only one who cares if we get in, and because I care so very much, I'm not at all worried. How could they possibly keep me out?

But they do. The handsome young man waits until I've had a good peek at the holy mystery inside the doors, and then the sign is in my face. On this sign is a line drawing, a woman in shorts and a sleeveless top with a ghost-buster circle and white line through it. I'm being thrown out because I'm wearing shorts? "But everyone in this line is wearing shorts," I start to protest. "It's a hundred and five in the shade!"

"Via!" he barks at me.

I can't believe this, not after the wait, the heat, the days of driving on the dangerous roads of southern Europe. "Who do you think you are?" I demand, and the Brit mutters sharply, "Hear, hear," so I crank up the volume, hoping to enlist the support of the crowd. "What's wrong with you? You can't keep people from going inside a *church*." Before the other pilgrims have figured out a revolution is in the making, however, my husband takes me by the arm and hustles me off, our embarrassed offspring trailing behind us.

I am, of course, furious. "He was completely out of line," I protest. "I couldn't let him throw me out without *saying* something."

But Michael, named for an archangel, is stripping off his white polo shirt, wet with sweat, and pulling it over my head. "There," he says, stepping back and surveying me. "Now you're fine." I look down at myself. His sleeves come down below my elbows. The bottom edge of his shirt falls to my knees. Instead of the verboten shorts and sleeveless blouse, I am now wearing a polo shirt dress.

"Get back up there," he says. "Don't wait in line again. Go up to the other guy and he'll let you in." I look at him doubtfully. The sun glistens on his chest hair. Our kids have skulked off, pretending they don't know us.

"Go on," he urges. "You know I'm not into churches anyway."

This is true, a sad gap between us.

I gird up my polo shirt and slip back into the pilgrim river, popping up silently as a fish before the second guard, who looks me over and starts to wave me through. The first guard, however, glances over at exactly the wrong moment, and I can see his brows lower; not only has he recognized me, one of the day's more memorable troublemakers, but he's spotted me cutting into the line. He plunges across the barricade, leaving his side unmanned, and I watch ten lucky souls slip through the doors behind him as he comes my way. But I'm *Catholic*, I wail (a big lie) as he shunts me aside.

However, I am not one to admit defeat. Avoiding poor half-naked Mike, who has found a good dozing spot in the shade of a building, I track down my oldest, who is always a good sport. I whisper my secret plan in her ear, then haul her around to the left side of the church where, in a recessed portion of the church wall, is an open door, hidden by a thick velvet curtain that hangs motionless in the heat. When we peer inside, we find ourselves looking at banks of flickering tapers and petitioners on their knees: a dim side chapel. The curtain conceals another police barrier. "Come on," I whisper, and we clamor over the cold metal and are in.

For a moment I stand staring up at the magnificent ceiling of the main rotunda, delighted with my own derring-do. Off to the right, pilgrims are making their way toward the heart of the vast building, the tomb itself, and though I am tempted to head straight there, I decide to stop a little and pray, a rather sanctimonious decision, considering the circumstances. I give my daughter a reassuring look (she has taken up a post near the velvet curtain, nervously shifting from one foot to another) and arrange myself on a kneeler. No sooner have I closed my eyes, however, than a rough hand seizes my shoulder, shakes it, pulls me to my feet. It is him, and this time I'm done for.

He thrusts three fingers before my face, as if to say that this, my third violation, places me in the class of incorrigibles, the class of those who, for all eternity, will neither pray at St. Mark's tomb nor enter the gates of Heaven. For just a moment I see myself the way that the kneeling petitioners, most of whom are surreptitiously watching all this, must see me: a pushy American with neither dignity nor hope of redemption. For a moment, I am awash in shame. But then he hisses something contemptuous in Italian and fury takes me once again. I flip him off in Catholic, crossing myself so aggressively that he can't miss the message. I say, knowing he doesn't speak English, "If we were on a bus, you'd be staring down my blouse, you hypocrite." He takes a threatening step toward me. I say, as though this will change his mind, "I came all the way from California to see this."

"Caly-*fornia*," he says, drawing out the "for" the way you would in "fornicate," and fake-spits on the cathedral paving stones. In this gesture is contained his immense disgust for the blight that is Hollywood, for beaches and bikinis and the idols of commercialism that are worshiped by his Euro-suave Italian brothers and sisters, for the rebellious American Catholic church, for the tourists who daily desecrate his sanctum. If he could, he'd throw me bodily back into the street.

But this time it is really over. I give him one last defiant glare and scramble back over the barricade, my humiliated daughter behind me. Then my fury collapses and I am crying, blubbering into my husband's polo shirt in the middle of the Piazza San Marco, wondering if there is, after all, a scarlet letter emblazoned across my chest, invisible except to the watchdogs of the Church. Wondering if the door will always be locked against me.

Many people don't realize that it is difficult to become a Catholic. I certainly never anticipated that my bid to enter the Church would become a vastly tangled affair that eventually required the annulment of my first marriage and a second wedding ceremony with Mike, who had already put in a good number of years as my legal spouse. In some vague, hazy way I assumed that Vatican II had ended "all that"—that the Church no longer much concerned itself with people's "private lives," those areas of our existence, specifically the bedroom, that we late twentieth-century individualists firmly believe to be "off limits," nobody's moral business but our own.

My ignorance in this line was rather typical, I believe. People outside the context of lifetime Catholicism take note of the big events: the Pope visiting Mexico, the disgruntlement that sometimes flares within the ranks over the not-yet- and maybe never-lifted requirement of priestly celibacy. Outsiders are willing to concede that Catholicism is a mysterious religion, full of odd, incomprehensible ritual, but they tend to interpret this mystery as simple confusion, sorted out and pared down later by the Protestant reformers. Others are less restrained in their criticisms. These folk may find religion itself rather harmless, more of a yawn than anything else, yet something about Catholic worship raises their ire; something about it morally offends and disgusts them. For such people, the rituals may call up the complex, at times downright nasty history of the Church-in-the-world, or its refusal to accommodate certain basic facts about *how things are* these days. They may symbolize an antiquated patriarchy (priests, bishops, cardinals, Pope—all those *men*). However, such folk—and I used to be one of them—rarely conjecture about whether or not they could join if they wanted to. The Church is so enormous, after all; how can you explain a billion members without an open-door policy?

And so it was a great surprise to me to discover that the Church does indeed bar the gates at times, that joining the Catholic church is not necessarily a matter of personal choice.

"Surprise," actually, doesn't quite describe that discovery. The day I was told that I would have to drop out of the Rite of Christian Initiation for Adults (RCIA) program and seek an annulment before the Church could consider allowing me to participate in the sacraments as a full-fledged Catholic, I felt shock, pure and simple, in the sense of "the shock of the icy water took her breath away." Like many Americans of my generation, I'd never before run up against the kind of authority that places the integrity of institution over individual "rights." Along with shock, of course, came the simple human anger of being rejected, which erupted months later in those shamed tears at the door of San Marco.

As someone who had been AWOL from church for many years—not only AWOL but utterly faithless—a serious reassessment on my end was now in order. The important thing, I thought, was God. I'd finally found him again; I didn't want to cloud that trembling, delicate new clarity on things. Did I really need corporate religion? Could I stick with this admittedly rocky new spiritual path without the inspiration of liturgical worship, sacrament, the warmth of a congregation shuffling in their pews around me? I knew that others had done it, at least for a while—religious geniuses like Paul, Francis, Teresa of Avila, George Fox. Yet their times of solitude all seemed to lead back to the same place: roles of leadership in the new, more vibrant version of the Church that grew up around them. Many of us, it seems, need the visceral unity of group worship, the shared symbols of "organized religion," the spiritual grit of religious discipline, the (at times) daunting authority of institution. I was afraid that if I tried to go it alone, I'd be tempted to take the path of least resistance, to create for myself a relationship with God that, more than anything, pleased and reassured me. Worse, that allowed me to remain aloof and critical.

My decision to proceed was not so much brave as it was desperate. I'd found something that spoke directly to the crying need within me and did so in ways that I could not command, surprising ways that kept me off balance, less apt to think I was running the show on my own. True, I could have gone to another church, an "easier church," as they put it in RCIA, "around the corner." But an easier church might not do the job, might not be able to tame this thing in me that needed taming.

Though my own effort to become Catholic was complicated by the annulment procedure, my experience was not unique in one regard, which is that the Church takes you in when it wants to take you in, and not before. And the reason for this delay is that you need to know what you're getting into. You need, the Church believes, to understand the rituals that so intrigue, confuse, or horrify the non-initiate, and you most definitely need to know what you are doing when you partake of the Holy Sacraments. For this reason, would-be Catholics must go through a nine- to twelve-month catechumenate modeled on the lengthy "apprenticeship" undertaken by first- and second-century converts.

Before my abrupt departure from RCIA, I got some explanations for what I'd already noticed: that the sacraments lie, in some very deep way, at the heart of Catholic worship. According to the *Catechism of the Catholic Church*, the sacraments are " 'powers that come forth' from the body of Christ, which is ever-living and life-giving." They are continual reenactments of his life among us: "What was visible in our Savior has passed over into his mysteries." Twentieth-century theologian Edward Schillebeeckx explains them this way: "What Christ alone did in the objective redemption, although in our name and in the place of us all, he does now in the sacraments."

These rituals, I was told, are "efficacious signs"; not only do they stand for something of tremendous import—the absolute victory of love over evil—but they cause certain internal changes in the participants. According to the *Catechism*, "they bear fruit in those who receive them with the required dispositions," and this fruit is "both personal and ecclesial." Those who partake of the sacraments, in other words, receive in a special way "the grace of the Holy Spirit" and "the Spirit heals and transforms those who receive him by conforming them to the Son of God."

Thus, when Christ says in Matthew 5:48, "You must be perfect as your heavenly Father is perfect," this is not the kind of lofty-sounding idealism of which our age is so suspicious but a loving injunction to transform our pathetic, meager lives, to infuse them with new power. This enabling grace of which the *Catechism* speaks, though it can certainly come in a myriad of startling, individual ways, is available in a particularly intense form through the sacraments. Historically, Catholic belief in the centrality of the sacraments led to what nowadays seems like an odd, even suspect, form of worship: one that involves repetitious physical acts and codified oral responses, one that emphasizes the group encounter with Christ over, say, Luther's individual experience of God.

That this difference in focus helped make for a definitive split between Catholics and Protestants was made clear to me early on. I was raised in the Lutheran church and didn't leave it until my early thirties, at the time of my divorce, though of course I'd said my private farewell to God long before. As a child I absorbed the anti-Catholic prejudices of the mostly Midwestern congregation in which I grew up. I picked up the notion, for example, that Catholics worshipped idols and that they elevated their Pope higher than God. I was shocked to find out that they had to have as many babies as they could produce, whether they wanted them or not, or they'd be excommunicated, a mysterious term that gave me a nervous thrill. I was left with the conviction that Catholics were simply, hugely wrong, that they'd gotten off the track around a thousand years ago and were now headed, two-by-two in those frilly white confirmation dresses of theirs, straight to hell.

What I grew up with was a dim, folkloric version of the original violent clash of the Reformation. And to some significant degree, the Reformation was about the sacraments. Both Luther and Calvin, for example, went to war with the long-held Catholic belief that the sacraments were effective in spite of the mental state of their participants at any given moment—or, as the Church put it, *ex opere operato,* which means "by the work having been worked." The reformers sensed grave danger here: the possibility that the uncomprehending faithful might take Church ritual for magic. And certainly this was (and still is) a justifiable concern. The Church, as Evelyn Underhill reminds us, receives and conserves "all the successive deposits of racial experience, it is the very home of magic." The modern Church has bent over backward, some say too far, in its effort to avoid misusing its supernatural power.

Another major concern of the reformers was that the sacraments could act as impediments to a genuine, heartfelt, individual relationship with their Lord. Though Calvin retained Baptism and Eucharist, what moved him far more was the "personal dialogue between the believer and God," and he fought what he believed was a tendency to "convert the Supper into a dumb action." Certain later groups went so far as to drop the sacraments entirely—the Quakers, for example—and others (the Evangelicals) emphasized the need for an emotional "sense" of God's presence as a way to counteract what they feared had become rote ritualism.

So when the door of the Church came creaking shut for me that night at my RCIA class, it should not have been a surprise to me that the issue at stake was a sacrament. Though my first marriage, at nineteen, was a Lutheran one and Luther refused to recognize matrimony as Christ-ordained ("Not only is the sacramental character of matrimony without foundation in Scripture; but the very traditions, which claim such sacredness for it, are mere jest"), ironically enough for me, the Catholics believe that Christian marriage, whether it takes place before a priest or a Protestant minister, is indeed a sacramental covenant and constitutes an "indissoluble bond" that cannot be broken without spiritually serious repercussions. I was stuck, unable to move forward, until the Church could view the facts, discuss them in light of its doctrine, then make a decision about whether or not to grant me an annulment. This, the priest told me on the day I decided to go ahead with it, "could take a long, *long* time."

The San Marco debacle felt, obviously, like an instant replay of that memorable night at RCIA. However, no matter how these double rejections rankled, deep down I knew that, given my history, they were probably no more than I deserved. Recently, in fact, a writer friend who knows about my past laughed out loud when I told him the San Marco tale, then quickly apologized. "Sorry, sorry, couldn't help it, but—how perfect. The guard won't let you into the church because of your sexy California shorts, but of course what he *doesn't* know is . . ." He trailed off, no doubt after a tardy realization that he was making a hurtful joke at my expense, but after a while I heard him chortling quietly to himself in the kitchen.

Though he'd managed to start an old scar aching, I understood. Sex *is* often funny, especially when it doesn't involve oneself. It's funny in its fleshy, urgent animality; it strips us of our pride and exposes us for what we are: "half beast, half angel," as Bishop Berkeley put it, or creatures with one foot in the "Zoological Garden." When we're in the grip of mighty sex, we're drunkards; we're like, as Proverbs says, "one sleeping on the high seas, lying on top of the rigging."

Later, when we come to, we say wonderingly, "I lost myself," and this is not so funny—that it is possible for an otherwise fully functioning, intelligent human being to so completely cut loose. Renaissance poets, in fact, referred to sex as "the little death." We do get a preview of death, or at least earthly carnal death, through this temporary annihilation of the thinking self. And this vacation from reason can even be a relief, a kind of pseudo-mysticism. Or, instead of flirting with oblivion this way, we go to the other extreme, try to fortify ourselves against death by clinging to the flesh of another. In our desperate yearning, we can become downright voracious, heedless of Simone Weil's warning that when we try to "eat" beauty, to eat what we love, what we eat "is destroyed, it is no longer real." Either way, however, at the brink of the little death we never feel more stupendously alive—so it is understandable that through the centuries, and in our time especially, we have been tempted to worship sex. Or at the very least, to construct elaborate and lofty self-justifications for indulging ourselves in it.

For a number of years, for example, I was convinced that adultery was not really adultery if it involved "genuine love." And because of this self-serving belief, during these same years I lived a double life: the first, a useful, respectable, cheerful one as wife and mother; the other, a fevered and ecstatic one as clandestine lover of another woman's husband. And all this in a small town where families regularly met one another at Farmer's Market, met again at the soccer field, again at PTA, again at the choir concert in the high school gym. For years I hummed with a high-pitched, glittering energy that sometimes and without warning would entirely drain out of me; all I could do at those times was creep into bed for a few days, sick of body, sick of soul. Otherwise, I was fully occupied with an impossible task: to maintain not just the appearance but the actuality of the first life, the normal, good life, while not giving up a single stolen moment of the second.

The inevitable explosion, when it finally came, flattened everything for miles around, a far greater swath of destruction than I'd ever, in my few rational moments during this lunatic time, allowed myself to imagine. Everything I valued lifted off the ground, turned over and over in that fiery, furious air, then fell back around me in pieces. Eventually, however, Mike and I refound each other in the wreckage. He'd lost his little girls; I was now a half-time mother. We two former celebrants were sober and exhausted, weighted down by the knowledge that what we'd so unthinkingly set into motion could not be stopped—that what we had unleashed would insinuate its way into the lives of our children and we could not save them from this.

There ensued a long shame-filled interlude, the shame made more acute, no doubt, by the small-town stage on which all this was taking place. Eventually, we married, did our best to start over as a so-called "blended family," but this sunny term in no way describes the dark reality of what we were facing, nor does it describe the tentative, guilty parenting of these early years. An interesting fact about shame, however, is that it cannot go on forever; something has to give. If I'd been open to religion then, I might have sought out a priest for confession, penance, absolution, but given my lack of faith, this seemed the height of hypocrisy. Instead, I tried to get rid of the awful burden by turning it back on the people we had wronged.

The seduction into self-righteous rage is as insidious as the seduction into lust, and often has more deadly consequences, because at the heart of it is the urge to destroy. "External Reason supposes that hell is far from us," wrote Jacob Boehme. "But it is near us. Every one carries it within himself." The first custody petition was filed innocently enough—no matter what we had done to their mother, Mike had the right to see his daughters, after all—but when she responded by hiring a criminal lawyer, the battle was engaged, a violent acting-out of her need for retribution and ours for an enemy. After numerous court appearances, probation reports, mediation sessions, and private counselors, however, we had very little to show for any of it. Mike's visitation times were regularly blocked, holidays were a nightmare of tension (would we get them or wouldn't we?), and worst of all, the poor girls had been hounded into a state of permanent distrust. The legal bills amounted to $55,000, money that we obviously didn't have and had to borrow, but the true price, of course, was inestimable.

When I first talked to the priest about an annulment, I told him just a little of my story, just enough for him to get the picture, and I said, hopelessly, that I could not imagine going back into a courtroom of any kind, not even one conducted by priests. He told me that he understood, but that the purpose of annulment was not to pass judgment on the divorce, but instead on whether or not one was capable of making the decision to marry in the first place. A number of conditions—coercion, mental illness, drug or alcohol addiction, even pregnancy—could impede or even invalidate one's ability to enter into a lifetime covenant. I would have to write an account of my life during my teenage years, and I'd have to find five witnesses who knew me then. My ex-husband would be offered the chance to respond. The priest explained that annulments granted by the Church in no way change the civil status of a marriage: Our two children would not lose their status as legal offspring, and the thirteen years we'd spent raising them as husband and wife would be in no sense "erased." The tribunal would instead focus on whether or not the "indissoluble bond" part of the relationship could be set aside so that I could complete the catechumenate.

The decision to divorce and all that led up to it, he added, were instead matters for confession. *Serious* matters for confession. He asked me to think very hard once again about why, after all this, I'd come to the door of the Church and then to decide whether or not this longing constituted a genuine call, a call compelling enough to resurrect such a painful history for all involved.

This was an important question. For what he wasn't saying out loud but no doubt thinking was, How is this, your fervent desire to join the Church, any different than your other fervent desires? How do you know that this is not simply a new version of the same old impulsive pattern? The answer was that I honestly *didn't* know. I still couldn't sort out very accurately what was moving me from the outside and what was moving me from within. And until fairly recently my life had been driven by a "complete and ungraduated response to stimulus—an all-or-nothing reaction," as Underhill puts it, to whatever impressive thing happened to cross my path. This instinctive reaction that knows no bounds can give the illusion of great power, and certainly in my life as a fiction writer, I'd learned to rely upon it. The critical and controlled had always seemed in comparison weak and boring, the antithesis of the rich and creative. Yet this Romanticism of mine was, I now knew, key to the mess I'd made of my life. Curiously, it was a re-quired college course that spurred this important revelation and led, ultimately, to a search for the God I'd scorned so long ago.

I am sitting in a classroom, a living cliché: a woman in her late thirties finally trying to get a degree. Not only do I crave the educa-tion, I find that focusing on my studies is a good way to distract my-self from the custody situation. My professor is lecturing on Hume, something to do with a great breakthrough he made in the—what was it? the eighteenth century? I'm trying my best to take good notes but I'm yawning and nearly asleep where I sit. After all, I'm not only a full-time student but a mother of four (I always put it this way, never mentioning that two are my seldom-seen stepdaughters), a wife, a university library employee, a writer. I'm doing my best, I think defensively. This is something I often do: defend myself to myself, as though I were two people in terrible disagreement. I struggle to pay attention, but so far this business—modern ethics—is dryer than dry. Then, however, my professor says something that makes my head come up. "What Hume was pointing out," he says, "was a simple thing no one had spelled out quite so explicitly be-fore, and that is the gap between 'is' and 'ought.' "

This arrests me, for some reason, though at first I'm not even sure what it means. I look up Hume's own words on the subject:

> "In every system of morality which I have hitherto met with I have always remarked that the author proceeds for some time in the ordinary way of reasoning and establishes the being of a God or makes observations concerning human

affairs, when of a sudden I am surprised to find that instead of the usual copulations of propositions, *is* and *is not*, I meet with no proposition that is not connected with an *ought* or an *ought not*. This change is imperceptible, but is, however, of the last consequence."

I think about this, trying to figure out why it is so disturbing. What he is asking, I decide, is how we justify our morality. And I don't have a clue.

I go back and read earlier selections in the book—chapters on shame and honor, on teleological views of human nature, on virtue and vice. I'm thirty-eight, and I've never heard any of this until now, yet it is somehow familiar to me as my own heartbeat, like a native language long since forgotten. I want Hume to be wrong, I want there to be an anchor for goodness that's stronger than, as he puts it, "habit and convention," and I'm surprised at myself for wanting this so badly, considering where I've been in the past few years. Oddly enough, however, I would rather believe I've been contravening some venerable, weighty, pure law of goodness than simply flying in the face of arbitrary social mores.

I take more ethics classes, all from the same professor, mostly because I am too embarrassed to trot my ignorance before anybody else in his department. I read bits of Plato, Aristotle, Augustine, each making me more miserably aware of two problems: the depth of my ignorance and the confusion that reigns in my moral life. When I am not taking a class, I am asking questions. I can't seem to get enough of this business: It is as though I have been thirsty for years and am finally being offered an unlimited supply of fresh water, even though there are times this water burns going down.

The day arrives when I begin, almost without noticing it, to bring my own life into these discussions, and I realize that I have developed an urgent need to get better, to *be* better, though I'm not even sure what I mean by this. Almost in spite of myself, however, I am undergoing a different kind of "little death." I can feel the props beginning to give, the comforting fantasies to evaporate, but beyond this I can see nothing. Later, I will read John Ruysbroeck's description of this moment: "We behold that which we are!" Now, however, I am simply terrified. What will I be when all this stripping away is over? A cipher? A zero?

I confess some of this to my professor, who, because he has heard it many times before, knows how to listen and what not to say. He does assure me that I am not alone, that countless human beings have been down this road before me. I tell him how frightened I am, that I don't believe I have the courage or strength to change myself no matter how I want to. I tell him I wish I could believe in God, that this would probably help, but I can't, I gave up God when I was seventeen. When he asks me why, I tell him, a long litany of accusations based on a rebellious adolescent's misreading of the Gospels. He says, "There's a way to read the Bible that doesn't make God out to be a fool."

A year later, I am still struggling, but in a different way. I've accepted my professor's challenge—I've studied Christ's words—and what they've given me is a radiant vision of genuine goodness, genuine love. Radiant, but depressing, for given my nature, they seem utterly out of my reach. Though there will come a time that I can read and comprehend Saint Teresa's admonition to her daughters ("If you seek by force of arms to bring it to you, you lose the strength which you have"), I have not yet figured out that the more I flail away on my own, the further back I slip. I have not yet seen, as Boehme did, that "because thou strivest against that out of which thou art come, thou breakest thyself off with thy own willing from God's willing."

I'm sitting in a pew in the local Catholic church, where I sometimes come to think about these things. The light is very bright high up where the windows are, softer below. The old white adobe walls, bulging fatly here and there, look soft too, not like the cold gray stone of the big European cathedrals, but homespun. The pews are simple, straight-backed, uncomfortable, green, scarred by a couple of centuries of schoolkids' surreptitious carvings. One of Father Serra's California mission churches, San Luis Obispo de Tolosa, established in 1772.

This time I have not come to sit but to meet my professor's wife. I've met her before; she's lovely and shy, and I like her, but this feels strange to me, as though I am being rushed into something, even though it was my idea. He's told me about her; she sounds different from anybody else I know—*better* is perhaps a more appropriate word. She goes regularly to a monastery up the coast, she has monk friends, she says the rosary, all of which sounds unbelievably medieval and compelling. The truth is I am looking for a model, for living proof that we really *can* be transformed. I'm sure, however, she doesn't suspect what I am up to and would no doubt be nervous if she did.

In the sanctuary are the usual types: a couple of old Filipino women with sparse black curls messing with an altar bouquet that's bigger than they are, a homeless human metal detector cruising the center aisle for loose change, a janitor tossing burned-down candles into a plastic garbage bag. And then I spot her, three rows back. Both of us, out of nervousness maybe, are early, and she doesn't suspect I've arrived, so she's taking this opportunity to pray. I stop and stare, never having studied a person deep in prayer before. She's down on the kneeler and her eyes are closed, and in the diffuse light with her head tipped slightly that way she looks beautiful, but I am impatient with this purely aesthetic judgment for it doesn't begin to capture what she seems. Then I see what makes her so unusual: her utter stillness. She has gone somewhere with someone she loves and they are conversing in private and she will have to haul herself back into this world when she is done.

If I leave right now, I think, I will have gotten what I came for, which is proof that people really do this, really live this way, with one foot in two realms. And the secret path is prayer, its worldly fruits the love and the goodness I so crave. Later, I will see this explained by the famous Indian Christian, Sadhu Sundar Singh: "Prayer is as important as breathing." Later, I will find the writings of Saint John Chrysostom: "Nothing is equal to prayer; for what is impossible it makes possible, what is difficult, easy." Now, however, I'm simply arrested by this stolen glimpse of a woman talking with God.

Later I understood that this moment was a turning point for me, for shortly thereafter I began to go to morning Mass—at first, mostly out of curiosity, for I knew nothing about Catholicism, this religion that seemed to have so powerfully shaped my professor's wife. I kept to myself and took my cues from the other early morning faithful. Much of what went on was physical, which at first surprised me; I hadn't thought religion had much to do with the body. There was a dancelike rhythm to it—genuflect, kneel, stand, kneel—that felt choreographically wedded to the liturgy.

Slowly, as the ritual became less alien to me, I found myself missing it when I couldn't be there, wanting to be present even though I couldn't participate. I saw that the center of Mass is the Eucharist, that Communion is the fulcrum around which everything else turns. For a long time I was too shy to go up, instead kneeling in my pew with head down and eyes closed, listening to the shuffle of people moving past me, the priest intoning, "The body of Christ, the body of Christ, the body of Christ." For some reason, the hush, the shuffle, the chanted words always made me cry, and I sensed that this had as much to do with the physical, the presence of the faithful around me, as it did with the spiritual presence that hovered over us like incense. Underhill describes this phenomenon well: "It is one of the most beautiful features of a real and living corporate religion, that within it ordinary people at all levels help each other to be a little more supernatural than each would have been alone."

Inevitably, the day arrived when I joined the throng, crossing my arms over my chest when I got to the raised plate of bread, as I had seen other non-Catholics do. For several long moments I stopped breathing as the priest leaned forward to give me his blessing. This, too, made my heart swell and weep, and I was amazed that this sacramental stuff could sweep me around so powerfully, even as a nonparticipant on the periphery. Later I came to believe that certain kinds of pain, deep deserved guilt being one of them, lie beyond the reach of analysis or assurance, perhaps beyond language at all, and that this silent, aching place can only be touched through a physical and spiritual acting-out, a ritual infused with grace.

All this, then, is what I thought about as I pondered whether to pursue the annulment. Some people, people I cared about, would be upset. Most wouldn't understand. My conviction, however, was that my life, the only one I'd ever be given to live, would be a better thing if it took place inside, rather than outside, the Church, and so I filed the petition. After eighteen months, however, the tribunal had not yet made its decision. I didn't know if my case was a particularly difficult one or if they were just overwhelmed with divorced people, but I kept going to Mass anyway and tried to remain hopeful. Besides, a year and a half of crossing my arms during the Eucharist was having an odd, helpful effect on me: I was finally up against something I couldn't manipulate, cajole, threaten, or deceive into complying with my wishes, and I was learning that my will and its demands were not paramount. I could even think of the San Marco cathedral guard with some (certainly not yet wholehearted) sympathy. Strangely, the Catholics, by keeping me out, had done more to shore me up than any amount of reading Plato or Kant had ever been able to do. Maybe, I thought, the sacraments had a reverse gear that took care of nonparticipants like me. Or maybe the more significant moral lessons got learned when you put your body on the line as I did each time I made myself, in public, stand before the priest only to be turned away.

One day one of these priests called me, a man with whom I'd never had a conversation before, though he'd often enough blessed me during Mass. Father John asked if there was some reason I was not taking Communion. I explained, and he promised to call the tribunal himself to see where my case stood by now, all of which made me feel amazed and hopeful. When he got back to me, it was to pass on the word that there were more questions on their way from the Diocesian offices, which duly arrived and which I answered. His third call, several months later, brought me the long-awaited happy news: The annulment had been granted.

"You're *kidding*," I said. "On what grounds?"

He hesitated. "Gross immaturity?"

I laughed.

"But that's true of a lot of people," he assured me. "Especially at nineteen."

I was grinning into the phone. "What happens now?"

"First your ex-husband has an automatic appeal. If he chooses not to respond, the decision becomes final in several weeks. Then you and your current husband—Mike, isn't it?—will have to remarry in the Church." There was a pause. "Mike has never been married before, has he?"

Sudden dark silence. I thought of the thousands of dollars in attorney's fees, the nightmarish and tempestuous years when our life had been one with hers. "Yes," I said very quietly. "Yes, I'm afraid so."

Father John paused. I could hear his own disappointment in the long interval. Finally: "I don't suppose he'd be willing to go through the annulment process himself?"

"No." I said this flatly. Mike did not want to be Catholic, had in fact found my growing devotion to the Church a profoundly unsettling bit of business, and there was no way, given our history with the civil court system, I would even ask. "No, Father, that's it, I'm afraid. If they're going to require that, I can't go any further." I felt somewhat numb, as though I'd just taken a hefty blow to the back of the neck, but for once not like crying.

"Paula," said my kindhearted friend. He'd never addressed me by my first name that way before; it sounded curiously intimate and had the effect of comforting me. "There may be a way. I'm going to look into it. Don't lose faith, please."

At some point in the weeks that followed, I reread Mark's account of the feeding of the five thousand, Jesus so adeptly rearranging the molecules of five loaves and two fishes that everyone in the place gets a full meal plus extra—surely one of the more stupendous miracles on record. Later, and in spite of having so recently served as the miracle feast clean-up crew, the disciples have once again worked themselves into a state of high anxiety because their stomachs are growling. Jesus says to them, "Why are you talking about having no bread? Are your hearts hardened? Do you still not see or understand? Do you have eyes but fail to see, and ears but fail to hear? And don't you remember?" I thought about the bread of the Eucharist, the Body of Christ, given up for me, and the fact that though I might be forever banished from the table, I was still one of the hungry crowd. And that the Jesus I'd read about in the Gospels always, in some way, fed the hungry.

Father John finally called back. "There's a way," he said, "if you are willing. It's called 'internal forum,' and it allows a priest to use his own best judgment in certain special cases." He waited for me to say something, which I didn't, then explained, "I think it would be better for one of you to be taking Communion on a regular basis than neither of you. That's my judgment." He stopped again, but I, for some reason, was suddenly thick as mud. He said, "Mike would have to agree, in front of me, to be remarried in the Church, and nobody could attend but your children and two witnesses. On that day, you'd become a Catholic. What do you think?"

A week later we assemble in the Old Mission Church on a Saturday afternoon: my husband, the kids, and (unsurprisingly) my professor and his wife. Father John seems happy to see us, happy that this long project is finally drawing to a satisfying close, and he signals me to follow him back into the sacristy for a moment so that we can talk alone before the small ceremony begins. There, among the hanging vestments, the half-burned candles, the big sinks that are used for washing out communion goblets and wafer plates, he confesses that he's not completely sure of the ritual required in this circumstance—that normally all this is done on Easter Vigil with the rest of the catechumens in a fairly lengthy and elaborate program that involves bare feet, white robes, etc., and that we have, at this moment, none of this at hand. Not even so much as a congregation in the pews. We scratch our heads—somehow, we've reached an anticlimactic moment without meaning to—and then he says, "What about the Apostle's Creed? Can you say it from memory?"

This, for the average Catholic, would be the equivalent of a curveball, since it is the Nicene Creed that gets recited in Mass and not its shorter, blunter brother. However, my Lutheran childhood now saves me, for when it comes to creeds, the Lutherans prefer to get right to the point. I dutifully recite the lines that begin, "I believe in God the Father Almighty, Maker of Heaven and Earth, and in His only Son, Jesus Christ...." and with only a little stumbling, declare my faith in the "Holy Catholic Church, the communion of saints, the forgiveness of sins, and life everlasting." Father John and I look at each other. "Amen," I add firmly. He nods, then traces a cross on my forehead with his thumb, blessing me the way he's blessed me for nearly two years now, and then we break into mutual grins, and I hug him. "Thank you," I say into his robe, "so much." He nods, pats my shoulder, then steers me toward the small door beyond which my husband, children, and friends wait for us in front of the altar.

And thus I go through the marriage ceremony for the third time, shivering a little inside, as I did both times before, at its awful weight and portent. The first vow, made when I was only nineteen, seems, in spite of the tribunal's declaration of annulment, still a curiously living thing, a shadowy, uninvited guest at this present ceremony, as though the bond between people who have borne children together is not severable. I think of Saint Augustine's declaration that "when man and wife are once united by marriage . . . as long as both live, there remains something attached to the marriage, which neither mutual separation nor union with a third can remove." I look up at Mike and wonder if he is being visited by his own ghosts.

In preparation for this day, I have read about the sacrament of Matrimony and its long history, the fact that it was not officially, in print, recognized as a sacrament until the beginning of the thirteenth century. I learned that the chief ends of this sacrament—which is unique among the seven sacraments in that it is conferred by each spouse on the other rather than by the priest—are "to enable the husband and wife to aid each other in securing the salvation of their souls . . . to propagate or keep up the existence of the human race by bringing children into the world to serve God, [and] to prevent sins against the holy virtue of purity by faithfully obeying the laws of the marriage state." These are noble ends, worthy ends, but unfortunately condemn by their very worthiness and goodness the vows we are about to make, for Mike, at this point in his life at least, is little interested in the salvation of his soul, I am biologically incapable of bearing more children, and we have already violated, in our previous lives, the laws of the marriage state. I begin thinking gloomy thoughts, which fortunately Father John interrupts with his opening blessing: "In the name of the Father, and the Son, and the Holy Spirit, Amen."

We few Catholics present at this little ceremony make the holy sign—forehead, heart, left shoulder, right shoulder, heart—giving ourselves over with an anticipatory sigh to the incoming, outgoing tides of the Mass. The reading is from Revelations, the "wedding feast of the Lamb," and I glance past Mike's profile (he is listening hard) and catch my professor's eye; he winks at me, and in that twinkling wink is an acknowledgment of all the long and convoluted history behind my standing before this altar, this priest, this great crucifix hanging from a white adobe wall. Father John says, looking straight at me, "The sacrament of Matrimony gives the husband and wife grace to bear each other's weaknesses. They must be patient with each other's faults and bad habits, and forgive one another easily, just as God forgives us every day." I think of all I have been forgiven and of the inevitable new heap of crimes and misdemeanors, the dross and fallout of intimate human relationships, that lie ahead for Mike and me. I think that one of the many disciplines of marriage may indeed be daily, mutual forgiveness, and I wonder if I will ever be capable of practicing it. Father John says, "The power of marriage is that you can help each other overcome these faults by being mirrors for one another. When things become difficult between you, remember that the sacrament imparts special grace to help you through."

These are stunning words, *special grace*, and I know that he doesn't mean them metaphorically. According to the sacrament of Matrimony, we are now something more than the sum of two shaky human beings occupying the same space and trying to make a go of it. I love this idea, I want to hang on to it, but it's like jumping for handfuls of mist. Instead, our little ceremony ends, the kids give us somewhat dubious hugs, we all go out for frozen yogurt. Before taking up our normal, nonsacramental lives once again, we stop for a single group wedding photo on the bridge over the creek beside the Old Mission. And that's it. I'm Catholic, duly married in the Church, and all, I think, will now be well.

✳   ✳   ✳

A long tradition that begins with Paul in Ephesians uses marriage as an analogy for the relationship between Christ and his people: "Husbands, love your wives, as Christ loved the church. He gave himself up for her to make her holy." (5:25–26) Then he adds, "For this reason a man shall leave his father and mother, and shall cling to his wife, and the two shall be made into one. This is a great foreshadowing; I mean that it refers to Christ and the Church."(5:31–32) At the time Mike and I remarried, I had a better understanding of the spiritual half of this equation than I did the human. For in spite of the long years we'd already shared, we'd not yet caught up with one another, and our history still dogged us, shadowy but real. Without realizing it, I wanted "one flesh" to mean "one person." I wanted Mike to stop "hanging back," to quit resisting the urge I thought I could discern in him toward confession, penance, absolution: *my* path.

Instead, we entered a bleak time, the bleakest in our marriage, and ironically this hit just when everything else finally calmed down. Three of our four kids were in colleges out of state, and the last, busy with her final years of high school, rarely came to see us anymore. At first this was nice—we could breathe, look around—and then it got very quiet, and then it became frightening. Our house began to feel like a cheerless, childless sepulcher. I caught Mike giving me surreptitious, sidelong glances, heavy with doubt, as though he was wondering what on earth ever possessed him to go to hell and back for *this*. We started not sleeping. We both lost weight. Mortified, we realized we'd become weary of one another's company at the very moment everyone had gone off and left us alone together. We began to bicker, to squabble, to pick, this unhealthy practice becoming so second-nature so very quickly that we were both taken aback when our oldest daughter pointed it out on a visit home at Christmas. "What's up with you guys?" was how she put it, confirming that we had somehow managed not to tear at each other through all those truly awful years (court, police, child counselors) but now were. This was embarrassing and had alarming undertones.

Then one day I went alone to the wedding of a friend, a good-sized Catholic wedding at the Mission. I caught the groom for a hug before he went to take his place beside the altar, and he whispered to me that chaos could break loose, that one of the more volatile homeless women had wandered into the church earlier that day and torn most of the wedding bows off the pews, threatening to come back. I laughed and told him not to worry, he had bigger things to think about right then. For the fact is, we all know this woman, know how obnoxious she gets, and we are proud to belong to the kind of church that lets her through the door in spite of this. The notoriously tough institution that so warmly offers Christ's universal love. I sat in the pew where I'd sat so often, and I watched my friend and his bride, both of them young and handsome, free of the webby ghosts that Mike and I will always share, as they made their public covenant. Who knew what they might face together in the terrible intimacy of matrimony? And then it came to me that faith in a marriage is a small analog to faith in God, and that I had somehow forgotten this. I had somehow sealed my marriage off from the rest of my spiritual life and come to the grim conclusion that it was up to me, and me alone, to fix whatever had gone wrong. And I asked for an infusion of that special matrimonial grace I'd forgotten about for so long.

Things slowly seemed to heal. Where, for a while, there had been a frightening void, there was once again something bigger than the two of us—the sacramental combination Father John had told us about. As much a part of each of us as a limb, and not nearly so expendable. It was a start, and I was grateful for it, grateful that though for a time we'd been strange and appalled with one another, we now seemed to be rediscovering, like long-lost cousins at a family reunion, our common root.

But, like the loaves, like the fishes, there is much more on the way, a scene that comes one day while I am walking, so vivid in its details it seems a waking dream. In it, I see us and what we might be, what is meant for the two of us together in this mysterious thing called marriage. I see that there is a way to harness our "fiery energies" to the "service of the light" and that, as Augustine shows us, it is the right ordering of the still-present love and desire between us that will lead us into virtue. Virtue, of course, being nothing else but the ancient name for the power of goodness, the tremendous power of the Holy Spirit who enters when he is invited. I see that what I once dared only hope for is after all a glorious reality, open to every one of us, regardless of the darkness through which we have passed. And I finally know for certain that "All will be well. All will be well. And every kind of thing will be well."

SOURCES

Paul Althaus, *The Theology of Martin Luther* (Philadelphia: Fortress, 1966).

Thomas Bokenkotter, *Dynamic Catholicism: A Historical Catechism* (New York: Doubleday, 1992).

John Calvin, *Institutes of the Christian Religion, Vol. I.* Trans. by Henry Beveridge (Grand Rapids, MI: Wm. B. Eerdmans, 1953).

Catechism of the Catholic Church (New York: Doubleday, 1995).

The Catholic Encyclopedia (New York: Robert Appleton, 1914).

Frederick Copleston, S.J., *A History of Philosophy, Vol. VI.* (New York: Doubleday, 1994).

Council of Trent, Twenty-fourth Session, "Doctrine on the Sacrament of Matrimony," 1613.

Pope John Paul II, "Pope John Paul II on Marriage: the Redemption of the Body and the Sacramentality of Marriage." General Audience of November 28, 1984.

Evelyn Underhill, *The Life of the Spirit Today* (London: Methuen, 1922).

HOLY ORDERS

MURRAY BODO, O.F.M.

Good Friday, 1948. I am standing on the front step of my house. The muslin chasuble blows in the New Mexico wind. In front of me kneel seven children, boys and girls, Anglos and Mexican-Americans. I am inviting them to rise and come forward for the adoration of the cross. I am eleven years old.

Between that histrionic performance—and all the "Masses" I "said" as a child dressed in vestments my mother made for me at a "play altar" with its own little tabernacle draped in lace curtains—and the Mass I offer this morning at Pleasant Street Friary in Cincinnati, lies the story of my priesthood. I look at another old photograph of me playing Mass at a makeshift altar in the rented house on Fifth Street in Gallup. It looks strikingly like the makeshift shrine in my room here. We are who we were.

I can't remember when I didn't want to be a priest. There was a time, of course, when I had other images of what I would be when I grew up. There are, for example, photos of me "cooking" as a three-year-old in Silverton, Colorado. I'm standing in the backyard snow with pans all around me. Then there are the snapshots of me in cowboy boots and Levi's, a white Stetson hat scrunched down on my four-year-old head. I'm at the Bodo ranch in Durango, Colorado. I don't remember those times, though I remember the World War II soldier times when I was six or seven, but by then the image of myself as a future priest was the most vivid picture in my imagination.

This was before the Second Vatican Council, so the image invoked fiddleback Roman vestments, a marble Romanesque altar. In this imaginary photo, I am standing with my back to the congregation, reading the Mass in Latin. Other priests are offering Masses at the side altars that line the walls of the church; at the rear on each side of the church are confessionals we enter every Saturday. In my child's mind, the whole ambit of priesthood somehow arced back and forth between altar and confessional.

Why, I wonder, is offering Mass so vivid a picture? Did it have something to do with the theater of it all? In a small New Mexico border town in the early 1940s, the priest at the altar must have seemed special, so removed from the mundane, blue-collar lives of coal miners and railroad workers. The gold-brocaded vestments alone would have fired an imaginative young boy's dreams. Then there was the respect the priest was given in our Mexican, Spanish, Italian, Croatian world. He was somehow elevated, different, worthy of emulation.

Or was it something magical, mystical? The dizzy feeling of kneeling in the small church of St. Francis of Assisi in Gallup, thinking it was huge because I was little, overcome with the scent of lilies, the swirling incense, the profusion of lights and candles washing the altar cloths whiter, the priest in his gold vestments for Christmas or Easter, his chasuble sewn of spun gold, his shoes polished bright, his hair as white as his alb starched stiff and proper by the white-wimpled sisters.

The ecstasy of it all—like a young athlete caught up in the rhythm, the movement of a Michael Jordan setup and shot, or my father listening on the radio to Joe Louis box. That identification with the ideal. You are the priest ascending for the first time the altar of God, caught up in the dynamic of what you admire and love.

And so it probably began, the first inkling of a vocation, later to be clarified and solidified when I began in junior high to drive the car for the Hospital Sisters of St. Francis who had come west from Springfield, Illinois, to minister to the poor sick and shut-ins. Through these sisters the image of Saint Francis working with the lepers took shape in my mind, and I knew that I, like the priests and sisters in my hometown, could only be a *Franciscan* priest who would one day live among the poor. That, too, has come to pass, though life in inner-city Cincinnati looks different from the 1950s images I had of living a Franciscan life with the poor.

Though in some ways generic, the memories of a priest's seminary days and those of his priesthood are unique to him, to the way God prepared him for ministry and the way he has chosen to live out that ministry in the Church. The time of my own leaving for the seminary is an image of war in Korea, of Dwight Eisenhower as president, of the McCarthy era just beginning, and of me reading Thomas Merton's *Seven Storey Mountain*. Though I was only fourteen years old, Merton's book held me enthralled. All the places he had seen and where he was born and the Kentucky monastery where he was living seemed like faraway, fairy-tale places to a boy growing up in New Mexico, longing to travel, to experience what he'd read about. I rode the bus out of town as on a white and gleaming steed to conquer in myself and others the Evil Enemy, just as Francis of Assisi had ridden into battle against Perugia, the neighbor and enemy of Assisi. He rode forth to master and destroy the evil that was coming at him from "out there" somewhere, from outside himself.

Perhaps this accounts for my not thinking twice about the geographic and emotional distance between Gallup and Cincinnati. That is what you did in those days if you wanted to be a priest—you went to the high school seminary, wherever it was. And everyone congratulated you and was proud of you, except maybe your parents who tried desperately to understand but still thought it was too soon to leave home. They were probably right—as parents seem to be in the long run. But I would hear none of that. I was in love with the idea of becoming a priest and wanted to give my life to God.

Though my roots were in the American Southwest and, before that, in Northern Italy on both my mother's and father's sides of the family, I eagerly embraced the rather Prussian regimen of the seminary because it so perfectly suited what I was about: becoming a saint by erasing my past, putting on the garments of penance, and embarking, with the earnestness of youth, on the long and arduous journey to the mountain of God. Asceticism itself became the god I'd hoped to meet on the mountaintop.

I set out, as spiritual manuals urged, by mortifying my palate: no desserts, no overeating at table, no eating between meals. It is not my rather priggish moderation, or even the mortification of the palate, that amazes me so much today as the extremes I went to in trying to be moderate. Somehow from the pious literature I was reading at the time, I became convinced that if I yielded to even the smallest pleasure of the palate, I would fall into other sins as well.

Such asceticism could have made my adolescence a miserable, tortured time. But strangely, it was not. It was filled with the sweetness of spiritual consolation and deep love for Mary, the Mother of God. I spent hours before her altar each week, and I lived in a world of incense and stained glass and countless Lives of the Saints that I read avidly, the way teenagers usually read comic books. Spiritual books were the real depository of God for me. They held God, and if I could only enter them, I would enter into God.

I didn't expect to find in churches what I was looking for, because what moved me, was real for me, was the printed word. Books drew me the way the Blessed Sacrament of the Body and Blood of Christ drew a saint into the Divine Presence. For me, almost literally, "In the beginning was the Word." And that Word I had first found in a book. I wonder how much of *The Seven Storey Mountain* I understood back then? Rereading it now, I'm sure I must have missed most of the references Merton makes to contemporary events, people, literary works, including the title's allusion to Dante's *Purgatorio*. What I did understand and what kept me reading was that Merton's words were of God. The one who wrote them had found the God I was looking for, the God who preoccupied me.

But God is not confined to books and the feelings they evoke in us. This a priest must know, and this God taught me in the only way I could learn. My troubles began when I entered the novitiate and began the retreat prior to donning the habit of Saint Francis. I had prayed for this moment, prepared for it, all through the high school seminary years when most other teenage boys were learning about relating to girls, about living in "the world." However, it was at the retreat that all consolation ceased, all religious sentiments, all joy, and I was left without the felt presence of the God I thought I carried in my back pocket like the books that made God present to me.

It was then that God began the slow process of rebirthing me. I began to experience that dark night of the soul I'd read about and could so glibly assent to intellectually as a way to closer union with God. But now my resistance to this "self-sweat of spirit," as the poet Gerard Manley Hopkins names it, all but drove me mad. I was convinced I was spiritually arid and psychologically depressed because I had done something sinful, that I hadn't done enough penance, that God was angry with me; and so I increased my penances, unwilling to admit that maybe this was God's work, that God was leading me to a deeper relationship with him in the only way that I would hear.

The light of my spirit went out. Eventually, I began to read again, not *books*, but *authors* I trusted; and the more philosophically and theologically "sound" they were, the more I trusted them, though never did I give myself over into their power as I had those other writers of my boyhood like Saint Thérèse of Lisieux, Saint Louis de Montfort, Thomas à Kempis, and the early Thomas Merton. I analyzed authors now and argued with them and tested everything against my own experience of the "absence" of God in my life. God was revealed in sacraments and the Word. Period. It had nothing to do with feelings. God was not a "spiritual experience." You just believed. You didn't try to stir up enthusiasm by reading pious literature; you read books like Dietrich von Hildebrand's *Liturgy and Personality*, Dom Chautard's *Soul of the Apostolate*, Romano Guardini's *The Lord*.

Faith was all. Faith was gift. But what had taken place within was a subtle substitution of an intellectual world for the world of the emotions, the world of mind for the world of sentiment. However, the mind proved to be only a further escape, more subtle, more dangerous than the previous illusion that strong feelings indicate the presence of God's grace.

A dogmatic, doctrinaire attitude more often than not reveals a repressed personality rather than a person certain of his or her convictions, a self in hiding rather than a self firm in a given faith. I thought, for example, that I was pure and chaste, and in one sense I was, but for the wrong reasons and certainly not in a healthy way. Instead, I was becoming asexual. I, like others before me, was deceived by my own self-anointing. My own mind's "orthodoxy" had led me away from a lived orthodoxy, which is always incarnational, always about men and women, not angels. I did not know it then, but I needed to become a human being before I could become a real disciple of Jesus Christ, the *incarnate* Son of God.

What I praised about the sacraments, their merging of matter and spirit, I denied myself. Bread and wine became the Body and Blood of Christ and remained bread and wine in appearance and taste and function, but for me body somehow had to become spirit before it was holy.

This is an extreme way of stating what I lived and believed at that time, and had anyone asked me, I would never have given intellectual assent to such a Manichaean stance. But on the day-to-day level, that attitude was informing my action and nonaction in a way I would have been ashamed to admit.

Of course, in a "remembrance of things past," we are selective about what and how we remember. The years of my preparation for the priesthood were not wholly preoccupied with the fear that I would never again find the God who fled my books and was now somewhere in hiding. Other things were happening as well, and the work of God within me and around me was having as great an impact on my daily life as were my own fears and whatever else was motivating me in a conscious, compulsive way. I was following the schedule, doing what my spiritual directors assured me was the only way to proceed in spiritual aridity, namely, pray and work as if you felt the presence of God. If I persisted, they told me, God's presence would return. This *modus vivendi*, they all agreed, is the test of true love of God: to love God for God's own sake and not for what God can do for you; to persevere in spiritual discipline despite the lack of any feeling or consolation. This is the supreme detachment for one seeking the face of God. And so I continued to fulfill the offices of a once passionate love that I no longer felt. During the following four years at Duns Scotus College in Michigan, I submitted to the daily routine of the rather monastic horarium.

Through all my college years, faith alone carried me through, faith, especially, that I wasn't just putting in time and would never move beyond this arid plateau on which my spirit was marooned. My anxiety arose from the fear that I was going nowhere spiritually. I wanted the vows to lead somewhere, prayer to go somewhere, but I saw pride raising its head again and I fortunately listened this time to my spiritual directors rather than passages in books. I surrendered to what seemed an empty routine, I kept what seemed empty vows; and paradoxically that surrender led to God's return, just as my mentors had said it would.

In giving myself over to the daily routine of our Franciscan life, I was embracing the wisdom of centuries of spiritual formation. And since the ministerial priesthood is a way of life as well as a sacrament, I realized I must embrace my whole self, and not just a "spiritual" self. In so doing, I was given back, redeemed, everything I had feared was lost forever. As it turned out, it was Francis of Assisi who led me back, just as he had led me away as a boy, only this time it was through the famous leper story and not the would-be battle against Perugia.

One day while Francis was still living "in the world," he dismounted his horse and approached a leper standing shamefaced in his path. Though, like most people, he was nauseated by the sight of this disfigured person, he embraced him anyway. Immediately, his own heart was filled with joy, and he was no longer afraid; and as he mounted his horse to leave, he turned to wave, but there was no one there. He realized he'd embraced the Lord Himself in embracing the rejected, the marginal person. Furthermore, in embracing the leper, Francis was also embracing what he was afraid of in himself, what he had not yet reconciled in his own heart.

Through Saint Francis, then, I realized that what God was showing me throughout my boyhood and early youth was that I was my own leper, that I needed to embrace myself before I could embrace others.

Nor was this transformation just an intellectual exercise; it was made in the body, my own body and Christ's. It meant being able to look at myself in the mirror—not just from the neck up as in a "head trip," but my whole self in a full-length mirror—and seeing there that I was made good and beautiful in God's sight. Not just to see, but to celebrate what I saw.

The reality of the Incarnation had become real for me. What I'd known intellectually for years, I now felt in my bones, my blood, my heart. God is a flesh-and-blood human being, Jesus Christ. Jesus who had a body like mine, Jesus whose body is now glorified as mine will be if like him I embrace my whole self and love through it, with it. This transforming truth is, I believe, a *sine qua non* for the ministerial priest if his *life* is to be, in effect, a "sacrament," a sign of the sacrament of Holy Orders he embodies.

Even my prayer changed. Jesus was now a living, breathing human being whose feet I kissed, with whom I conversed, laughed, and cried. His wounds became emblems of my own previous fear and suspicion of the body which God made holy in His own flesh. The body was not separate from the soul, the body was enfleshed soul.

I stumble in trying to render that insight, that "epiphany" and the implications it had and has for how I now live and minister as a priest. I now *am* my body. It is the tangible expression of my soul, my immortal being, just as the tangible, human Jesus *is* the God whose essence and eternal being I cannot see.

After this transformative experience I felt as though Christ had somehow been awakened within me, as in this moving poem by Symeon the New Theologian, a Greek Orthodox abbot, theologian, and poet, who died in 1022.

> We awaken in Christ's body
> as Christ awakens our bodies,
> and my poor hand is Christ, He enters
> my foot, and is infinitely me.
>
> I move my hand, and wonderfully
> my hand becomes Christ, becomes all of Him
> (for God is indivisibly
> whole, seamless in His Godhood).
>
> I move my foot, and at once
> He appears like a flash of lightning.
> Do my words seem blasphemous?—Then
> open your heart to Him

and let yourself receive the one
who is opening to you so deeply.
For if we genuinely love Him,
we wake up inside Christ's body

where all our body, all over,
every most hidden part of it,
is realized in joy as Him
and He makes us, utterly, real,

and everything that is hurt, everything
that seemed to us dark, harsh, shameful,
maimed, ugly, irreparably
damaged, is in Him transformed

and recognized as whole, as lovely,
and radiant in His light,
we awaken as the Beloved
in every last part of our body.

The dynamic of this poem is, I believe, the dynamic of God's working in every soul. The so-called spiritual life is *God's* work within us; our work is to respond to that Divine activity by trying to discern what God is doing within us, listening to the word God speaks in that action, and learning to love others by first learning to love ourselves as whole persons.

This may mean learning first of all to forgive ourselves. The story of my own inner journey to the priesthood is precisely that journey of self-forgiveness to self-love to love of others. It is the story of everyone who enters upon the inner journey to that center where God is "heard" in silence and solitude as transforming love calling us to love ourselves and others as God loves us.

It was only after this prolonged inner journey that I was ready—if anyone is ever ready—to be ordained a priest.

It is 1964. I can still feel his thumb, thick and firm in my palms. The smooth oil, slick with grace. My surprise at the soft flesh of this man ordaining me a priest. Surprise because he has spent two and a half years as a Japanese prisoner, a year and a half of house arrest after the Communist takeover in 1949, and twenty-eight months in a Chinese Communist jail. He was brought before a firing squad in a mock execution staged for cameras and propaganda, unaware of the ruse. He stood there in the blast of camera shutters, wishing he was with Jesus in paradise. And perhaps he was, from that moment on. How can I, kneeling here in the lull of all this soft sacramentality, even dream of emulating a living martyr bishop whose pudgy Polish thumb is signing me a priest forever?

I heard him speak twelve years before when I was a fifteen-year-old seminarian wide open for martyrdom and heroic sanctity. His voice, as he sat beneath the proscenium arch of the seminary study hall stage, came, it seemed to me, from deep within solitary confinement, from under a single light bulb, from the steady drip of water and the reek of a bucket of feces and urine—the sacraments of his personal crucifixion. He talked of how he mentally worked out logarithms to keep sane; that, and reciting all the poems he'd memorized as a young seminarian. No longer a prisoner, he still kept simple rules for health and happiness: *Talk less, listen more; look at TV less, think more; ride less, walk more; sit less, kneel more; rest less, work more; self less, others more; hate less, love more; eat less, live longer.*

But this memory is now eclipsed by the tangible moments of ordination: the anointing with holy chrism, a sign of the special anointing of the Holy Spirit who makes fruitful the priest's ministry; the presentation of the paten and chalice, the offering of the holy people that he is called to present to God; and the essential rite of the sacrament of Holy Orders, the bishop's imposition of hands on the head of the ordinand and the bishop's specific consecratory prayer asking God for the outpouring of the Holy Spirit and the Holy Spirit's gifts proper to the priestly ministry. And all of this grace mediated through hands that were once tied behind this bishop's back, through eyes that were blindfolded, as he prepared to die for the same Christ whose priestly ministry I am now entering.

We are at the liminal moment of the closing of Vatican II; the bishop's consecratory prayer is still in Latin. It loses something in translation, but even in English it continues to move me today, some thirty-five years later:

> Lord, fill with the gift of the Holy Spirit
> him whom you have deigned to raise to the rank of the
> priesthood,
> that he may be worthy to stand without reproach before your
> altar,
> to proclaim the Gospel of your kingdom,
> to fulfill the ministry of your word of truth,

to offer spiritual gifts and sacrifices,
to renew your people by the bath of rebirth;
so that he may go out to meet
our great God and Savior Jesus Christ, your only Son,
on the day of his second coming,
and may receive from your vast goodness
the recompense for a faithful administration of his order.

It is the almost physical memory of anointing and hands on my head and words heard in the heart that I live within now fifty years after I played priest. Sacraments are like that: physical signs that impart grace, which is mostly inward and profoundly spiritual. The physical is all we perceive; the spiritual is evident only in the metamorphoses that take place in our lives, the faith, the hope, the charity we cannot explain by means of purely human reason. The spiritual in the physical: God in bread and wine; God in water and oil; God in the consummation of married love; God in the anointing of the forehead of the baptized with sacred chrism in confirmation; God in comforting oil on the cool or burning forehead of the sick; God in the hearing of sins and in the words of absolution.

The Mass is the very center of a priest's life, the urtext of all the texts he lives by. He does not write the Mass; the Mass writes him. In the end the priest becomes the text he utters at Mass. His is the body broken, the blood poured out for God's people. The same is true for *all* who offer the Mass with the priest. It is their body broken, as well, their blood poured out. The heart of the mystery of the Mass is that each person's offering is subsumed in the eucharistic bread and wine become Christ, the perfect offering to God.

Because the ministerial priest is chosen by a unique ordination and consecration to preside at the table of the Lord, the priest bears a commensurate responsibility to become Christ the Priest, the one whose whole life is patterned after the Christ of the Last Supper, who consoles and prophesies, who breaks the bread and shares the wine with those at supper, who washes the feet of the Apostles.

The words of Saint Francis to his brothers who are priests ring in my ear:

> If the blessed Virgin is so honored . . . because she carried God in her most holy womb; if the blessed Baptist trembled, not daring to touch the holy head of God; if the tomb where He lay for some time is so venerated, how holy, just, and worthy must be the person who touches God with his hands, receives God in his heart and mouth, and offers God to others to be received.

And then, as is typical of Saint Francis, a paean flows from his mouth:

> Let all humankind tremble
> all the world shake
> and the heavens exult
> when Christ, the Son of the living God

is present on the altar
in the hands of a priest.
O admirable heights and sublime lowliness!
O sublime humility!
O humble sublimity!
That the Lord of the universe,
God and the Son of God
humbles Himself so
and for our salvation
hides Himself under the humble form of bread!
Look, brothers, at God's humility
and pour out your hearts before God!
Humble yourselves, as well,
that you may be exalted by Him.
Therefore,
reserve nothing of yourselves for yourselves
so that
He Who gives Himself wholly to you
may receive you wholly.

The ecstatic nature of Saint Francis's words may not quicken modern hearts, so desensitized have we become to anything less than the sensational: ecstatic words that pulse from the heart of mystery that some would like to explain away as the last gasps of an age of Faith.

And yet, and yet . . . it is the task and burden of the priest as we move into the Third Millennium to reaffirm mystery and ecstasy, to prophesy the coming of the Cosmic Christ in simple realities like bread and wine and ordinary human beings become Godlike through the same bread and wine become God.

The priest is himself one of the faithful. Moreover, he is ministered to even as he ministers; for all of the baptized are a holy priesthood among whom the ministerial priest is ordained to symbolize and do in a unique way what all the baptized do— make present the kingdom of heaven. The kingdom of heaven is within, and the unique sacramental, evangelizing, and prophetic role of the ministerial priest is to make the kingdom within visible.

When I played Mass as a child, I was putting on a minidrama that imitated what I saw the priest doing. Now when I offer Mass, I am presiding at God's reenacting of the whole mystery of salvation—the passion, death, and resurrection of Christ—in the transubstantiating act of bread and wine becoming the Body and Blood of Christ through the action of the Holy Spirit, who is always the primary actor in the sacraments.

Fifty years after I stood playing priest on the front step of our home, I stand at the altar of St. Francis Church, Gallup, New Mexico, where I sang my first Mass. They are still here, the Croatian, Italian, Spanish, Mexican, Native American faces that prayed with me when I was a boy. We are all graying, a bit slower, and I no longer assume a place above them as I stand before the altar. Neither is my back turned toward the congregation. We gather together around the altar as we offer this Mass in a shared priesthood we were all made more aware of by the Second Vatican Council. My ministerial priesthood is still radically different in kind from our shared priesthood, but their and my perception of how I exercise that priesthood has changed.

I am still liturgical leader of this gathering of the local church, but the emphasis is now on the sacrament of the Church itself, and not on the priest. How we relate is reciprocal to an extent that was unthinkable in 1948. These people who were then on the other side of the communion rail and sanctuary now stand in the sanctuary and proclaim the readings of the daily liturgy; they pronounce, "The Body of Christ," as they distribute Holy Communion; they take the Holy Eucharist to the sick of the parish. Some are ordained deacons who proclaim the Gospel at Mass and preach, who preside over funerals, who assist in the distribution of Holy Communion and in the blessing of marriages.

I find words for what I feel standing here today in Pope John Paul II's 1990 Holy Thursday letter to priests: "The priesthood is not an institution that exists alongside the laity, or 'above' it. The priesthood of bishops and priests, as well as of deacons, is 'for' the laity, and precisely for this reason it possesses a ministerial character, that is to say, one of 'service.' "

This represents an important shift. Very early in the history of the Church the distinction between clergy and laity appeared. By feudal times clerical society paralleled civil society, with its own courts, its own laws, its own officials. By the time of Pope Leo I (461) laity were referred to as *ecclesia discens*, the listening/learning church. Already in the sixth century the priest "said Mass" on behalf of the people; Mass was viewed as a sacrifice in which the Body and Blood of Christ was made present, was offered for the sins of the people, and was consumed in Holy Communion.

The Mass as it looked in the tenth century was the Mass I grew up with all through childhood, adolescence, and early manhood until my ordination and the advent of Vatican II: Namely, the Mass was a liturgy of sacrifice and supplication, rather than communion, thanksgiving; it was performed by a single priest and not by a bishop surrounded by his college of presbyters; it was done *for* rather than *with* people; it was spoken in Latin and not the vernacular. Also, by the Middle Ages the priesthood itself was increasingly bound to Eucharist—priests were ordained primarily for the celebration of the Eucharist. From the Council of Trent in the sixteenth century till today, the Catholic belief has been that ordination confers a sacramental spiritual power that permanently distinguishes the priest, and what he does in the sacraments he does by that power, and not by any delegation from the community.

The Council of Trent linked the priesthood even more to cult: *Sacrificium et sacerdotium ita Dei ordinatione coniuncta sunt,* Sacrifice and priesthood are conjoined by divine disposition. The great achievement of Vatican II in the 1960s was to liberate the priesthood from the limitations of this definition and to free ministerial service in the Church from being the exclusive prerogative of the clergy. It reintroduced the New Testament term "presbyter" for "priest." The term "presbyter" means "elder" and has more collegial and fraternal associations than does the term *sacerdos,* which means "priest." Vatican II still teaches that the eucharistic sacrifice is the center and root of the whole priestly life, and the real presence of Christ in the Eucharist is unequivocally reaffirmed, but the apostolic preaching of the Gospel convokes the people of God who offer themselves to God as a "living sacrifice." Through the ministry of presbyters the spiritual sacrifice of the faithful is made perfect in union with the sacrifice of Christ as the Eucharist is offered in the name of the whole Church.

In the midst of a Mass, an image rises in my mind: Moses, his arms supported by Aaron and Hur because "whenever Moses held up his hands, Israel prevailed; and whenever he lowered his hands, Amalek prevailed." (Exod. 17:11) This was a battle. It went well when Moses' hands were lifted in prayer. This image comforts me at the altar and in all my priestly ministry. I am a priest called from among the body of the faithful who are themselves priests. I am the one chosen to offer sacrifice and prayers with them. I am the visible symbol not only of their priesthood but of *the* Priest, Jesus Christ. But I am weak and sinful; I grow weary if not supported by the priesthood of all the faithful. I do not raise my hands alone—Aaron and Hur, Rebecca and Sarah, are holding up my arms. There is that reciprocity in the fullness of ministerial priesthood. The ministerial priest acts sacramentally in the person of Christ by reason of Holy Orders, the sacrament that incorporates one of the baptized into the order of those who, with the Bishop, continue Christ's mission of Priest, Prophet, Servant.

Another image, more disturbing, arrests my attention, something I've read in the *Selected Poems* of the Polish poet Zbigniew Herbert. The poem, "The Priest," is dedicated *to the worshipers of deceased religions.*

A priest whose deity
descended to earth

In a half-ruined temple
revealed its human face

I impotent priest
who lifting up my hands
know that from this neither rain nor locust
neither harvest nor thunderstorm

    —I am repeating a dried-out verse
    with the same incantation
    of rapture

    A neck growing to martyrdom
    is struck by the flat of a jeering hand

    My holy dance before the altar
    is seen only by a shadow
    with the gestures of a street urchin

    —And nonetheless
    I raise up eyes and hands
    I raise up song

    And I know that the sacrificial smoke
    drifting into a cold sky
    braids a pigtail for a deity
    without a head

No image distills for me so clearly the way I and other priests feel from time to time: that sense of despair and cruel comedy, that feeling that we are pathetic marionettes or clowns making absurd gestures at an altar whose God is, alas, no longer there, or at least no longer listening. We stand seemingly naked and vulnerable trying on the words that now seem utterly true and not just pious echoes of the words of the Savior on the cross: "My God, my God, why have you forsaken me?"

This image begins to dissolve into another that resolves Herbert's macabre image—macabre, but hauntingly true when faith yields to despair. I am walking the streets of Assisi one summer evening. I come around a corner and literally run into a little man who smiles and says, to my amazement, "I'm your brother Francis." I wonder momentarily if I have run into Saint Francis himself. In a way I have. His name is Francis but he is English—from Nottingham—and he is a diocesan priest, neither of which would fit the non-English, non-priest Saint Francis. And yet, as I am to learn, his is the spirit of Saint Francis pressed down and overflowing.

Years before, he came to Assisi to die; but while praying in the Basilica of St. Francis, he was given to understand that he was to throw away his pills and gather the scraps that fell from the Lord's table. And so like the stories of hagiography, he threw his pills away and waited for a further word.

One day (as legends often begin) he was walking the piazza in front of the basilica when he saw a young man dejected and forlorn, and he knew, as he had known before while praying in the basilica, that here was the scrap he was somehow to gather.

He went up to the boy and said, "I am your brother Francis. Come with me and I will show you how to pray." And so began Father Francis Halprin's real ministry, he who thought his ministry was over.

Several years and thousands of young men later, Father Francis found me, like all the others, in Assisi. He told me of his first conversion from a successful pastor to a man broken and suffering from an emotional collapse, shunned by everyone but his dog and a prostitute who brought him a meal from time to time. From emotional collapse to a subsequent physical collapse from cancer, he found his way back to Assisi, where as a struggling artist he had come as a young college student to study the frescoes of Giotto. A priesthood and a life away he returned to die and ended up caring for the scraps that fell from Christ's table, his "little brothers," as he called them, young men he would take in—five days at a time—and teach them to pray. His daily Mass at the Basilica of St. Francis, his prayer, his "little brothers." Such was his life until he died a few years ago in his eighties. Such is the life of any priest: his Mass, his prayer, his brothers and sisters to serve as the Lord himself shows him.

"No one showed me what I should do, but the Most High himself revealed to me that I should live according to the form of the Holy Gospel," Saint Francis writes in his last testament. That form of the Gospel, for the Franciscan priest or the Franciscan in spirit like Father Francis Harpin, is expressed by Saint Francis in the same testament: "While I was in sins, it seemed very bitter to me to see lepers. And the Lord himself led me among them, and I worked mercy with them. And when I left them, that which seemed bitter to me was changed into sweetness of soul and body."

The ministry of the Franciscan priest, whatever its external configuration—from pastor to teacher to chaplain to writer to administrator to preacher to whatever avocation his ministry embraces—is a ministry of working mercy with those who are or who perceive themselves as being on the margins, rejected, despised by others. These scraps from the Lord's table the Franciscan priest ministers *with* rather than *to*: "I worked mercy with them," Saint Francis says so tellingly.

The church where I most often work mercy today is a small arched chapel built of trust and listening and discerning. It is the church Jesus speaks of when he says, "For where two or three meet in my name, I am there among them." (Matt. 18:20) There are usually only two who enter this chapel, I and another person who has entered this sacred place to discern God's will.

Everyone who comes to me for spiritual direction already has a direction, of course, a configuration of his or her life, because of who their parents and ancestors are, where they come from geographically, what decisions they've made or failed to make, what they've suffered, and most important for this sacred relationship, why they've come for spiritual direction. Together we will discern the pattern of God's working in their lives up to this point, what it is they are seeking now, and what they are to do in order to respond to this new movement—where, in other words, God is leading them in the immediate future.

What makes spiritual direction doubly rewarding and important to me is that within this sacred space I am further empowered to make sacramental the sharing enacted here. If confession of sin is a dimension of the sharing, I am ordained to forgive that sin in the name of the One who dwells there with us. Because of this sacramentalizing of the person's sharing, there is the liberating knowledge not only that one has finally shared something profoundly personal in a sacred and safe place, but that one is forgiven.

It is Christmas morning. I stand at the altar in the chapel of the cloistered Poor Clare nuns. The altar is oak, beautifully crafted by one of our Franciscan Brothers. The chapel and monastery are in the woods of the former high school seminary I attended as a teenager and where I later taught for twelve years. It is a new monastery founded a few years ago. There are five Poor Clares gathered for Christmas Mass. A small group, a microcosm of the whole Church.

Through the large ceiling-to-floor windows that fill the entire convex wall of the sanctuary, all of nature seems ready to enter here. Deer cross nearby, and squirrels punctuate the silent oak trees.

All of creation is an immense sacrament. All created things are signs of God that we decipher in order to find our way to God. The medieval Franciscan theologian Saint Bonaventure put it this way: Every creature is a word of God. *Verbum Divinum est omnis creatura.* This is so because *the* Word, the second person of the Blessed Trinity, becomes one with all of creation in the incarnate Christ.

But in order to see God in all things we must see with a purified vision. The work, or practice, or *ascesis* of purifying one's vision, is characterized by medieval theologians as the threefold way of purgation, illumination, and union. In the Franciscan tradition that has formed me, this threefold way consists of recognizing and overcoming sin, imitating Christ, and surrendering to union with the Holy Spirit as the Beloved Spouse of the soul. These ways are recursive in the sense that each way is found within the others and intertwined with them. The soul is never fixed on a single way.

Nor is it possible or helpful to try and determine what particular way one is in. All three exist simultaneously, and the only marker I have found helpful is that one way seems to predominate at a given time in one's life. What that way is can usually be discerned like this: In the purgative way there seems to be a somewhat equal distribution of personal effort and God's grace; in the illuminative way more emphasis is given to the imitation of Christ; and in the unitive way the major component is grace, pure gift.

Another way of saying this is that souls are on three ways at the same time, ways that are beginning, progressing, and perfecting stages. As I see it, all three ways are operative in the reception and living of the sacraments. Baptism and Penance have much to do with the recognition and overcoming of sin; Confirmation, Matrimony, and Holy Orders enable us to imitate Christ in his ministry or to follow in the footprints of Christ, as Saint Francis puts it. Imitating Christ for Saint Bonaventure means living out one's life with Christ as the exemplar or template of how to live in the world as in a sacrament of the Divine.

The Anointing of the Sick and especially the Holy Eucharist are the sacraments of contemplation as surrender to union with the Beloved. In the Eucharist all of creation becomes sacrament in the signs of bread and wine. In surrender to the healing touch of Christ in the Anointing of the Sick, and in surrender to the action of the Holy Eucharist, contemplative union with the Beloved is attained.

The configuration of our inner life is the configuration of the lived sacramental life of the Church. And as that configuration reveals more and more the image of Christ in us and among us, we begin to see Christ in all of creation. We begin with the sacraments, we live them, we begin to see sacramental signs everywhere, we end up becoming ourselves "sacraments" of God's presence.

SOURCES

Catechism of the Catholic Church (New York: Doubleday, 1995).

Donald B. Cozzens, editor, *The Spirituality of the Diocesan Priest* (Collegeville, MN: Liturgical Press, 1997).

Patrick J. Dunn, *Priesthood: A Re-examination of the Roman Catholic Theology of the Presbyterate* (New York: Alba House, 1997).

Donald J. Goergen, O.P., editor, *Being a Priest Today* (Collegeville, MN: Liturgical Press, 1992).

Paul K. Hennessey, C.F.C., editor, *A Concert of Charisms: Ordained Ministry in Religious Life* (New York: Paulist Press, 1997).

John Paul II, *Holy Thursday Letters to My Brother Priests.* (Princeton, NJ: Scepter, 1994).

Czeslaw Milosz and Peter Dale Scott, translators, *Zbigniew Herbert: Selected Poems* (New York: Ecco Press, 1986).

Stephen Mitchell, editor, *The Enlightened Heart* (New York: Harper & Row, 1989).

Robert J. Wister, editor, *Priest: Identity and Ministry* (Wilmington, DE: Michael Glazier, 1990).

Anointing
of the Sick

MARY GORDON

It used to be called Extreme Unction. For years, I had no idea
what the words meant. I thought they were pronounced "Ex-
tree Munction," a confusion or elision similar to the one that
happened in the Pledge of Allegiance ("to the republic for
Richard Stans") and "Silent Night" ("Round Jon Virgin mother
and child"). In all three cases—the names of the sacraments, the
words to a patriotic pledge we all made every morning, hands on
hearts, the hushed evocation of the Christ child—the words
seemed simultaneously too important and too well known to allow a confession that you didn't know what they meant.

All lively religious traditions surround themselves with superstitions, and the American church in the fifties, whatever else it
had, had a sort of buzzing, triumphalistic communal life that was
a splendid breeding ground for lore. Many superstitions surrounded all the sacraments, and Extreme Unction, although in
many ways the least exciting rite of the seven, was no exception. It

seemed to carry with it the least sense of occasion; it was undoubtedly the least communal. You couldn't have an Extreme Unction party; there were no special outfits for it—you couldn't get an Extreme Unction dress the way you had a baptismal gown or a Confirmation outfit, or of course a wedding dress. Even the recipient of Holy Orders was vested for the first time in the accoutrements of his new life. There was nothing special you had to wear for Penance, but at least the verbs connected to it were active—you had to *go* to confession; there was the dark confessional with all its furtive, sometimes fetid secrecy, the screen between you and the priest, your hope that it was properly concealing. But Extreme Unction seemed to put the recipient in a radically passive state. It was the only sacrament that happened at home. Or worse, in the hospital. It was therefore disappointingly domesticated. Of all the sacraments, its recipients were the least bathed in glamour.

Except, of course, the glamour of being near death. And so the lore surrounding Extreme Unction was death-tinged, and the drama that this sacrament took on was the drama of emergency: the high tonality of the approaching end. When narratives rose up around Extreme Unction, they always centered on the priest, arriving (like a Mountie on a horse) in the nick of time. The dying one was always more or less faceless and anonymous, unless he (it was, somehow, usually a he) was a great, a very great sinner. There were *aficionados* of the sacrament, in the way there are people who like telling you the details of automobile accidents and train wrecks. These were often women who had some special access to clerical gossip (they worked in the rectory, or they knew someone who did). This gossip had its own diction. A typical sentence was: "Father got there too late; he had to give the guy conditional." Conditional absolution was given to people already dead. It was a mark of the unimportance of the participant's role in the sacrament that, in some of the more favored dramas centering on it, one part could be played by a corpse.

In the understanding of the time, one of the important things that a priest did was to be constantly available for a "sick call," or "the last rites," the popular name for the incomprehensible "Extreme Unction." Whatever time of day or night, whatever weather condition, whatever the priest's personal exigencies (illness, lack of sobriety), he had to show up. The sinner's eternal life depended upon it. I remember my mother talking about this demand as an explanation for the necessity of priestly celibacy. A priest's need to be constantly available for the dying meant he couldn't be available in the ordinary ways to a family. And besides, my mother said, what woman wants to put up with having her sleep interrupted all the time in the middle of the night?

In the popular narrative imagination, the last confession was the part of the sacrament that was focused on. Except, of course, there was the maternal/housewifely anxiety about having clean underwear in case you were hit by a car. You wouldn't want the priest to think you came from a bad home. But because of the nature of the sacramental practice, you had not only to worry about clean underwear, but also clean socks. Because the feet were anointed. And this was the part I fixed on as a child.

I didn't tell myself then—and it may be only a kind of false Proustification—that the reason I was right to be fixed on the detail of the anointing of the feet was that it was such a literal acting out of the mentality of sacramentalism. Our catechism told us that a sacrament was an "outward sign instituted by Christ to give grace." I can't remember that this definition had any meaning to me, possibly because the noun "sign" lacked what would seem to me a necessary prepositional explicator. Outward sign of what? Because we weren't given that necessary information, we missed the great genius of the sacramental life. Which is, precisely, to come to terms with—by sacralizing it—the corporeality of our life, with its fleshiness, its thingness, its comic insistence on the creaturely. The old blessing of the feet (the practice seems to be discontinued, and I think this is unfortunate, in the new rite) is an example of this insistence on the creaturely, with its inevitable comic tone. What is the most comic body part if not the feet? Oh, there is, "How beautiful on the mountain are the feet of the Lord." But toes are inherently funny. Not funny in a suggestive way, like noses or behinds. But innocently laughable. And to these were applied the sacred oil; this was the unction of whose meaning we remained perpetually in the dark.

The anointing of the feet was a part of the enactment of the impulse to cleanse the sinful body part, to forgive *it*, and the specific sins to which it specifically led the erring soul. It was clear to me what sins could be committed through the improper pull of the eyes, the ears, the tongue, the fingers—even, though to a lesser extent, the nose. But the feet? Was the Church, in its wisdom, asking forgiveness for our sins of restlessness, of disloyalty, of betrayal of our positions, of our desertion of our posts, of the wasteful practice of the love of change for its own sake? For our inability to be still when stillness is called for? For our urge to move?

Extreme Unction, then, took its power from its proximity to death. People who had received the last rites more than once were looked down on, as if they were a species of spiritual hypochondriacs. Priests would bring communion to the sick and hear their confession, but the special sacrament—the application of holy oils—was connected only to death. So the appearance of the priest was a cause for alarm; he was a stand-in for the Grim Reaper; everyone feared calling him too early. A priest I know reports that his visits at the hospital were not always welcome; family members were known to throw things across the room at the visiting priest, as if, by the violence of their gesture, they could keep death back.

The special name for the communion given to the dying was *Viaticum*, from the Greek, meaning "provision for a journey." Or, as a friend of mine translates it, "bread for the trip across the abyss." The host was carried in a special container, used only for this purpose, called a "pyx." The pyx, the stole, the candles, and the holy oils were carried in something called "a sick-call set," and this was considered one of the few appropriate presents to give a priest for ordination or for his anniversary. One can only imagine how many sick-call sets a priest had in his closet, like the multiple toasters of a newly married couple.

The words *pyx* and *Viaticum*, because their use was so specialized, so radically limited, shimmered in the vault of language—preciously arcane, brought out only occasionally, and only by the very few (and we were vain about the smallness of our ranks) who might know what they meant. Pyx, Viaticum, sick call, last rites, Extreme Unction, the last utterance of the reprobate or rogue, the sounds of ambulances or gunshot, the sight of helmets and bayonets, these were the images that surrounded the sacrament of the dying. Only the priest had a face, only he moved; the sick person was not a sick person but a dier. The messiness of long illness, the scandal of its endurance and the creativity of its destruction and decay, the sight of the prolongation of suffering—we were allowed to turn our eyes from these, rather than make them something with which the community had to reckon. There was only the priest, racing to the scene in his stole, heroic, single, unconnected to the living Church.

The part of the sacrament that had an impact on my life did not take place as a single, dramatic episode but as a series of repeated, almost identical domestic events, an ongoing process that was anything but operatic in its tone.

In 1961, when I was twelve, a newly ordained priest was assigned to our parish. That same year my grandmother developed colon cancer; she was told she had less than a year to live. She began the slow and drawn-out labor of her dying, and Father W., the newly ordained, brought her communion every week. He must have been twenty-four.

She lay in her bed, silent and stunned. A colostomy had been performed, so like a child, she had to be changed several times a day. The smell of the shit that came out of the hole in her stomach permeated the house, and I was never free of it. She had a series of small strokes that affected her ability to swallow, so a suction machine was installed to pull the phlegm from her throat so that she wouldn't choke. I felt as if I were watching a giant tree rot steadily from the blight that spread inside, a blight whose manifestation I could see in her: the red, raw bump on her stomach that had to be kept scrupulously clean.

Her archaic and iconic bedroom was transformed into an ordinary sickroom. Her bed with its iron bedstead was removed, and a hospital bed with bars and pulleys took its place; a series of tin tables with wheels replaced her wardrobe; these were covered with gauze and cotton and Vaseline and bottles of medicine, liquid, and pills.

Her smell, and the constant gurgling in her throat, nearly overpowered me. They were the atmosphere in which I lived. I had to give in to them, take them into my own body. I was saturated in them; they were too powerful for me to escape or to avoid. This was the atmosphere into which Father W. walked each Saturday, his young hair still damp from the shower, the smell of a too close shave still on him—male and healthy: Noxzema, Old Spice. He entered the atmosphere of the house like a scalpel cutting through diseased tissue. I almost didn't want him coming into our house, entering the stench and the heavy air of female decay. At the same time, his immaculate young maleness seemed to redeem and purify the air, which sometimes seemed to me literally unbreathable. When he walked in the door, his eyes lowered, the purple stole around his neck, reaching into his black pocket for the pyx that held the host, I felt a lightening of atmosphere that made me think there was some hope for my future life. But I was afraid for him: What was he giving up, bestowing this lightness upon us? What poison was he taking in?

He removed, by his presence, the tincture of death. But only temporarily. When he left, taking with him the gold pyx, now empty, that had held the host residing now in my grandmother's cancerous inside, the disease took over once again. We were the tenants of the estate not only of death, but of dying. My grandmother had lost the power of speech, so she would look at me with eyes that were first imploring, then furious if she wasn't understood. Every moment I was near her, I only wanted to run away as fast, as violently as I could. But I knew the saints would not have run away. I offered my terror to God, knowing you could offer anything to God, even your most unworthy temptations, so long as you didn't succumb, and he would glorify them.

My mother and my aunt felt I should be taught to change my grandmother's colostomy bag and to use the suction machine. As the months went on, they asked me to tend to her more and more frequently. Retching, I would dip rags into the tin blue basin by her bed. I undid the colostomy's complicated bandage with its twelve interlocking tails. I washed around her bump, then disinfected it. I rubbed Vaseline on her stomach and covered the area in gauze. I took a new bandage from the pile of clean ones and rebandaged her, weaving the tails securely so that there would be no leaks. It didn't occur to me to ask if I could be spared these jobs. If I didn't do them, everything fell to my mother and my aunt. And they were crippled with polio; I was able-bodied, whole.

Only Father W. seemed to notice that I had too much responsibility for a twelve-year-old. He asked my mother and my aunt if they thought it was right for me to be doing so much. My mother looked away from him, but my aunt stared him right down. "It's her grandmother, she loves her," my aunt said, in the tight voice no one could counter. Father W. gave up. I was glad he did; I knew he couldn't win, and an unsuccessful battle waged on my part would have been more demoralizing than a timely retreat. But I saw that someone was looking, that I was not, in my troubles, unregarded and unmarked.

He would try to speak to me when he came to bring my grandmother communion. But he was shy with girls, and I felt unworthy of his attention, so I was tongue-tied in his presence.

After he'd given my grandmother communion and returned the gold pyx to his pocket, my mother and my aunt buzzed around him, offering him food (which, unlike the other priests that came to the house, he never took), trying to get him to talk about sports the way they had with their silent brothers. But he always seemed eager to be on his way. "You know where to find me, any hour of the day or night," he said, and they believed him. I don't know what I believed. But I knew that while he was there, and for a little while after, things were better. The presence of grace was real, but short-lived; after a while it was swamped by the details of illness and her slow death. For a while, though, we felt more accompanied, and less alone. The family and the priest had a relationship because his visits were repeated. If our only connection to him had been a one-time anointing, the raggedness that comes when human life bumps up against symbolic practice would have been replaced by a singular clerical elegance.

This is a story that contains in it the imperfect connection between the ideal of the sacrament and the unseemly ragged edges of life as it seems to be most often lived. The desire to trade in the unseemliness of the sick and those who live beside them in their sickness for a more pristine, enclosed set of gestures is, of course, understandable, but it is an example of a characteristic ritual mistake. As the theologian Aidan Kavanagh notes, such practice reduces symbols to signs. "Symbols, being roomy, allow many different people to put them on, so to speak, in different ways," he has written. "Signs do not. Signs are unambiguous because they exist to give precise information. Symbols coax one into a swamp of meaning and require one to frolic in it.... Signs are to symbols what infancy is to adulthood, what stem is to flower, and the flowering of maturity takes time." It is also, as Kavanagh points out, potentially messy in the process. He warns against overindulging in the urge to "noble simplicity," as, in its desire for clarity of sign, it might press down the vital messiness that is the reality of the people of God.

It was in the interest of moving the sacrament of Extreme Unction out of an airless, if classier, clerical ghetto, into the messiness of the life of the seriously ill that Extreme Unction, as part of the liturgical reforms of the Second Vatican Council, was transformed from the sacrament of the dying to the sacrament of the sick. By moving in this direction, the Church was moving back to an older tradition, as it was only Charlemagne's attempt to make Christianity conform to a Roman ideal that moved the emphasis from the sick to the dying. Whereas in the first part of the eighth century, the Venerable Bede's references to anointing say nothing about preparation for death, by the close of the twelfth century, the sacrament had shifted its focus from the anointing to the Viaticum and was seen less as a remedy against sickness than a preparation for death. But it wasn't until the Council of Trent's *Doctrine on the Sacrament of Extreme Unction* that the suggestion arose that the recipient must be in danger of imminent death before receiving the sacrament. The Council of Trent, it should be remembered, occurred at a moment when the Church was feeling itself embattled; it was a response to the arrival of Protestantism, and in general, it set the tone for the fortress mentality that has been a continual plague on the faith and grace model of a church whose roots are, after all, in the gospel of Jesus. Although the council had important things to say about "the sacrament's effects as purification from sin as well as from the effects of sin, comfort, and strength of soul, the arousal of confidence in God's mercy, readiness to bear the difficulties and trials of illness, and even health of body where expedient for the welfare of the soul," it encouraged the delay of the sacrament until the last possible moment of life. It suggested that the unction should be, indeed, an extreme act.

The name Extreme Unction seems to have suffered a silent execution, which I personally regret. Despite Aidan Kavanagh's reported annoyance that the term "Extreme" was misleading in that it implied the last in a series, I find the somehow Americanized "Anointing of the Sick" a distinct second best, shorn as it is

of mystery, and even the cloud of obfuscation inside which creative misreadings can occur. But the impulse to put the sick at
the center of the ritual is exactly right. It takes away the curse
of what Simone Weil calls "affliction," by insisting that the sick
must be recognized and embraced as part of the community. The
impulse to banish the sick, to hide them from sight, to see them
as objects of revulsion from which the gaze of the healthy should
be averted, is a particular product of modern culture, and it adds
great burdens to the experience of the sick. Thus, we add to their
suffering the curse of affliction, a state which, Weil explains, is
made intolerable by its impersonality. "Affliction," she says, "is
above all anonymous, it deprives its victims of their personality
and turns them into things. It is indifferent, and it is the chill of
this indifference—as metallic chill—that freezes all it touches
down to the depth of their soul."

The oil of anointing warms and lubricates the metal of affliction; it disallows its power of freezing and cutting into the soul.
So the sick, having been anointed, are still the suffering, but they
are not the afflicted. Weil distinguishes between the two: "Those
who are persecuted for their faith and are aware of it are not afflicted, in spite of their suffering. . . . The martyrs who came into
the arena singing as they faced the wild beasts were not afflicted. . . . Affliction is ridiculous."

It is ridiculous because it partakes of the same mechanism as
the comic: It turns the person into an object. We can laugh at a
man slipping on a banana peel because we do not empathize with
him; he is ridiculous because we fail to put ourselves in his situation. We create a distance between us in which empathy cannot

grow up. It is this distance, this distancing that the sacrament of Anointing of the Sick makes impossible. At the same time, it makes no room for the revulsion that we often feel for the sick, when we turn them from the suffering into the afflicted. It is this revulsion that forces or allows us, depending upon our natures or our circumstances, to turn our eyes and our imaginations from them. We banish them as we banish criminals.

In forbidding the sick to be seen as types of criminals, in rather honoring them by the imposition of sacred oils, we remove all tincture of curse or blame from the condition of their illness. Above all, we insist that they remember that they are *us*, and we are *them*. They are *ours*, and we are *theirs*. In doing this, we take from them the burden of an illness that we cannot cure, an unnecessary burden. We take away the curse of their loneliness; we blast the superstitious idea that they are being punished for their sins. We honor them, as it is the genius of Christianity always to honor the poor.

In making the sacrament of Anointing of the Sick public, we allow all this to happen; that we deprive ourselves of the sheath-like simplicity, the easily legible drama of the priest galloping to the rescue is a small price to pay.

One of the dangers that the sacraments run, in the necessary amphibiousness of their marking of the connecting points of our physical and spiritual life, is that they can be turned into commodities. It is very difficult to avoid this, because in their commerce with the flesh, they are vulnerable to some of the flesh's more unglamorous sins: the desire for comfort, for preferment, for wealth, most important perhaps, for shortcuts. A sacrament should not be a shortcut, and it should not have a product, at least a visible one. It can use products—indeed it must— in the realization of its rite, but it must not itself produce anything that can be sold, or even used. In the Church's desire for legible symbolism, it cannot reduce its sacraments to a fineness of diction—verbal or gestural—that is untrue to the complex and contradictory nature of the living people of God. Aidan Kavanagh notes this tendency: "One cannot . . . think in a ritual context of the living and the dead . . . without soon realizing that human rituals are rarely short, clear, and without repetition. They are more often long, richly ambiguous, and vastly repetitious."

The Church diminished the role of the sick in the sacrament of Extreme Unction in an anxiety, perhaps, to avoid the spectacle of healing services, which might have called up, in older times, the specter of a pagan-based popular religion, and in modern times, the anxieties about hyperactive fundamentalism, both of these presenting the false promise of life and health. The promise of health is, after all, always eventually a losing proposition (even the early Christians died). Perhaps because of this, the Church excessively streamlined the sacrament. In the process it rendered the sick invisible and the priest hypervisible. It avoided the messy question—What is healing?—and its subordinate: Do the sick participate in the sacrament with the expectation of a physical cure?

The frustration of hope in a person already physically afflicted is a troubling and a grotesque sight, and the wish to avoid it is understandable. Such a sight was enacted in its more comic form in Fellini's *Nights of Cabiria*, in the scene where a group of pimps and prostitutes go to pray at a place where the Madonna was meant to appear. The pimps bring a crippled uncle with them, and in an excess of religious fervor, they urge him to lay down his crutches. He does and falls on his face. But in my experience, the expectation of literal cure usually proceeds more from those surrounding the sick than from the sick themselves. When the sick are healed, they are usually, first, surprised. I don't know enough about the connection of the mind and the body with healing to make a judgment about the relationship between belief and cure: All that I know is that the Church cannot be in the *business* of physical healing. Its healing must be invisible in order not to be corrupt.

The seemliness of the enterprise of healing is assured by the fullness of the ritual by which the sick are anointed. Most importantly, but not exclusively, by its language. The language and gesture of the sacraments work, when they work, because they are capacious, general, flexible, and resonant enough to remove them from the limiting specificity of one situation, time, or place. They must be simultaneously precise in their time and place, and yet have historical sweep; they must create a radical presence, or presentness, and yet evoke the sense that these words and gestures have been performed by women and men for many ages. The sacraments are about human life, but they are not about individual biographies. At the center of each sacrament is an act of worship; each sacrament involves the role of the individual in the worshipping community, a community whose very reason for its existence is the presence in it of God. It is the relationship between the lived life and the eternal one that makes up the form of every sacrament. As the liturgist Robert Hovda says: "When we do sacraments ... we create the atmosphere, the environment of humility and mystery and awe in which believers live their lives—a humility on our part that should make us supremely conscious of our commonness and equality as daughters and sons of God."

The language of the prayers of the new rite of the Anointing of the Sick succeeds in these sacramental/aesthetic goals with a remarkable grace and ease. Take, as an example, the prayer after anointing, "Father in heaven, through this holy anointing, grant (N.) comfort in her suffering. When she is afraid, give her courage, when afflicted give her patience, when dejected afford her hope, and when alone, assure her of the support of your holy people." The building rhythm of this prayer, its use of repetition that turns and turns and turns again, and thickens with each turning so that the ending—ushered in by the conjunction "and"—seems both inevitable and desirable, shows a mastery of the form that is both intellectual and physical.

Most people—and I, until quite recently was one of them—don't understand that this sacrament is constituted completely in the act of anointing, and that Penance and Eucharist are ancillary, and not necessary, parts. Anointing is an ancient custom, and its double role of healing and investing with power is an important aspect of the sacrament. It is a practice common to many peoples of the Near East, and the Church, in incorporating the act of anointing into its ritual, was inventing nothing and taking nothing generated from the Empire of Rome. Anointing means covering with oil; and oil, of all the substances used in the sacraments—bread, water, wine—is the richest and the densest. This is acknowledged in the prayer said at the time the oil is blessed: "Send the power of your Holy Spirit, the Consoler, into this precious oil, this soothing ointment, this rich gift, this fruit of the earth." It applies to the body a cultural artifact already produced by the body. The body produces its own oils; it does not produce its own bread and wine. Unlike water, it reminds us that we are fat, lubricious creatures. It coats the edges of things—distinctions are less distinct, separations less separate because of its unctuous flow. It picks up the light; it is golden, and it shines. Jesus is referred to as the "anointed one," signifying his messianic role, and this role is transferred to the sick in the Epistle of James where the elders of the Church pray over the people and anoint them "in the name of the Lord." Thus the sick are anointed, and the complex symbolism of this act invests them with a profound dignity: Their broken bodies are marked as sacred, and they are ennobled with the sign of kingship.

The new form of the sacrament is one of the unequivocal successes of the Second Vatican Council, and its very success, because it underscores the Council's unused potential, has a bittersweet taste. There were very few unequivocal successes, much that was gained has been lost, many difficult changes were avoided or balked, a great deal of the liturgical reform has not been met with the fervor that the council fathers had imagined. But the new rite of anointing is an example of a good that can come about when everyone is hoping for the same thing and no one's fears, hatreds, or phobias are creating a background noise. Perhaps this is because the sacrament of Extreme Unction never had anything to do with sex; it didn't threaten a male celibate establishment because none of its diction was made up of the words and phrases that spelt danger for them. The Church has always seemed much better at attending to broken bodies than to vigorous and desiring ones. It has been of much greater help to the faithful in guiding them towards the mystery of death than the mystery of life. The Church has a history of charity towards the sick and the dying of which it can be unabashedly proud; the corruptions of preferment seem not to have touched, in any finally damaging way, the ministry of the Church towards the sick and the dying, regardless of their wealth, position, or lack of it.

So the council fathers, in reforming the Rite of Extreme Unction, renaming it the Anointing of the Sick, were working from a position of strength or security. Nothing was embattled; there was no need for either defensiveness or accusation. There was not much struggle involved in this reform, and the laity embraced it because it met a genuine need and made their lives genuinely better. It was less vexed than the liturgical reforms of the Mass because the sacrament was less habitual, less a part of the fabric of daily life. It was a sacrament performed only in extraordinary circumstances, and it happened when people were most in need.

The letter written by Pope Paul VI to the Universal Church on 30 November 1972, outlining the new form of the sacrament, is a beautiful example of the thinking of the official Church at its best. It makes lively the sense of tradition and history; with ease it refers to the words of the Council of Trent, and their presence in a letter written five hundred years later has a freshness and liveliness that half a millenium has not tarnished. This is language that seems undiminished by time, unsubject to it, free of the browning or yellowing sense of antiquity or anachronism. It speaks of "the reality signified and the effects of the sacrament. . . . This reality is in fact the grace of the Holy Spirit, whose anointing takes away sins, if any still remain, and the remnants of sin; this anointing also raises up and strengthens the soul of the sick person, arousing a great confidence in the divine mercy; thus sustained, the sick person may more easily bear the trials and hardships of sickness, more easily resist the temptations of the devil 'lying in wait for his heel' (Genesis 3:15) and sometimes regain bodily health, if this is expedient for the health of the soul." The prayer that is meant to accompany the anointing is a model of liturgical elegance and simplicity:

Through this holy anointing
May the Lord in his love and mercy help you
With the grace of the Holy Spirit.

May the Lord who frees you from sin
Save you and raise you up.

The historical moment at which these words appeared adds to, or perhaps creates, the poignancy that surrounds them. Nineteen seventy-two was a low moment in the prestige of the Catholic church, and particularly the papacy of Paul VI. The pope's authority in the world had been fractured by his obstinacy on the issue of birth control (the 1968 encyclical was a scandalous moment in the history of the Church's moral authority) and, particularly in Europe and America, he had to face the reality of emptying churches, a disaffected clergy, many of whom were asking for laicization, and a larger world, which, because of the Church's intransigence in sexual matters, was perceiving it as an irrelevant moral force. Vatican II was seeming like an increasingly meaningless blip, something that had happened a while ago and was no longer really engaging to the imagination, a well-meaning but essentially failed effort, like the settlement house movement, perhaps, or Esperanto. The world was being torn apart by the forces of repression and resistance. Europe was reeling from the events of '68, and America was in a state of alternate mania and catatonia because of Vietnam and what had begun to seem like an endless string of assassinations. In this country, Paul VI was the butt of jokes among the movers and shakers: I remember a poster of him, his face furious, his finger wagging in our faces, and underneath it the words, "The Pill Is a No-No."

And in this time of upheaval, darkness, malaise, cynicism, and loss of hope, a nearly perfect document of its kind appeared over the signature of Paul VI. The statement on the new rite of the Anointing of the Sick calls up everything that is admirable and desirable about the Roman church, and nothing that is objectionable or scandal-bearing. With absolute ease, it reminds us of the straight line from Genesis to Rome, 1972; it affirms not only the Church's biblical roots but also its historical ones: The Church is part not only of sacred history but of the history of Europe. The document gets to the point of the required change clearly and simply; the emphasis is to be shifted from the sacrament at the point of death, a onetime-only offer, to a part of what can be an ongoing process of sickness and suffering. In acknowledging that olive oil may not be available in some parts of the world, it points to the reality that the Catholic church is less meaningfully Roman than in the past, that it is a global church, encompassing many cultures. It gives a specific time frame for the implementation of its rubrics; and it includes the minimum requirements for their effective carrying out.

It is an example of what Vatican II was meant to achieve, but rarely did: an accommodation to the realities of the modern world that was true to the history, spirit, and tradition of the Church. Of course, it would not be a media event; it was a family matter, like dealing with the care of an elder, not glamorous, not controversial, not even comprehensible to the outside world. Simply, it made life better for some people, and it did so by going back to a traditional source and enriching it with the communal history and wisdom of a vibrant organism.

The bedrock of this history and wisdom is the scripture, and the scriptural readings suggested for the sacrament of Anointing of the Sick bear witness to the richness and variety of text and tone that the liturgical genius of centuries can provide. The various needs of the human spirit are variously attended to by the range of possible scriptural passages. The Psalms provide the acknowledgment of a sense of wretchedness and abandonment. They join the sick at their most despairing and bereft, and provide, because of this, an assurance that others of their kind have, for centuries, endured these same hardships. The greatness of the

Psalms is their ability to meet the human spirit in its darkest moments, to accompany it, and to offer it a hope of deliverance based on the clearest possible look at all the realities, no difficulties elided or erased. In Psalm 6 there is the unvarnished cry from the depths: "Have pity on me, O Lord, for I am languishing; heal me, O Lord, for my body is in terror." In Psalm 25, the triumph of faith over affliction is evoked with great directness and simplicity: "My eyes are ever toward the Lord, for he will free my feet from the snare. Look toward me and have pity on me, for I am alone and afflicted."

The suffering servant of Isaiah expresses all the worst fears, with their tincture of self-loathing, that are part of the burden of illness. He is "harshly treated, he submitted and opened not his mouth . . . oppressed and condemned, he was taken away, and who would have thought any more of his destiny."(53:7–8) And earlier: "There was in him no stately bearing to make us look at him, nor appearance that would attract us to him. He was spurned and avoided by men, a man of suffering, accustomed to infirmity, one of them from whom men hide their faces, spurned, and we held him in no esteem." (53:2–3)

On a different plain from the impersonal grandeur of the Psalms and Isaiah, the example of Job, the just man unfairly stricken, provides a character with a face and a history, locating the experience of bodily suffering in a recognizable life. His words speak not only to physical hardship, but to the mental anguish that can accompany it: "When I say, 'My bed shall comfort me, my couch shall ease my complaints,' then you affright me with dreams, and with visions terrify me, so that I should prefer choking and death rather than my pains." (7:13–15) For Job, being in God's sight is not a help but a curse, and he prays, as many of the sick do, that the Lord avert his gaze so he can have some respite from its punishment. How clearly we hear his desperation when he cries out: "How long will it be before you look away from me, and let me alone long enough to swallow my own spittle?" (7:19) Yet the message of Job is one of steadfast faith, and he does not rest in his sense of aloneness: "I know that my Vindicator lives, and that he will at last stand forth upon the dust, whom I myself shall see: my own eyes, not another's, shall behold him. And from my flesh I shall see God; my inmost being is consumed with longing." (19:25–27) These words are the triumph of desire over despair; of the sense of connection over the sense of abandonment. They contain the justified pride of the one who has endured; there is the self-asserting repetition of the glory of identity: "I myself shall see, my own eyes, not another's."

In comparison to the high drama of the Old Testament, the relaxed narratives of the miracle stories from the Gospels and the Acts of the Apostles, with their leavening details—the stock in trade of the realist novelist—offer a kind of gossipy distraction and the comfort of story. It is a tale-teller, and not a lyric poet, who speaks when we hear of Peter's cure of the cripple. We know times and places; we know physical symptoms; we see behavior and gestural specificity:

> Once when Peter and John were going up to the temple for prayer at the three o'clock hour, a man crippled from birth was being carried in. They would bring him every day and put

him at the temple gate called "The Beautiful" to beg from the people as they entered. When he saw Peter and John on their way in, he begged them for an alms. Peter fixed his gaze on the man; so did John. "Look at us!" Peter said.

The cripple gave them his whole attention, hoping to get something. Then Peter said: "I have neither silver nor gold, but what I have I give you! In the name of Jesus Christ the Nazarean, walk!" Then Peter took him by the right hand and pulled him up. Immediately the beggar's feet and ankles became strong; he jumped up, stood for a moment, then began to walk around. He went into the temple with them—walking, jumping about, and praising God. (Acts 3:1–8)

In this account, God is in the details, in the feet, and the ankles, and the jumping. And a moment of great psychological truth enters when Peter insists that the man first look, take an active part, before his cure can become a reality.

The voice of Jesus, in its insistent personalness, provides a dialogue whose underlying theme is the assurance of accompaniment. "I am the Good Shepherd," "Come to me all you who are burdened," "I am the Bread of Life." The "I" of Jesus, with its implied "you" provides a text of relationship, a palpable connection with One whose loyalty is proved by his offering himself entirely, even unto death. And the example of this character, whose history unfolds before us in the Gospels, is an example of attentive service, an example that heartens both the stricken and those who minister to them. No voice could be less abstract, less distant, than the voice of Jesus in the Gospels. With every word there is the undercurrent, "You are not alone."

How different is the cool, intellectual voice of Paul, assuring our minds that we are right to believe. He says, in his letter to the Romans: "For I am certain that neither death nor life, neither angels nor principalities, nor powers, neither the present nor the future, neither height nor depth, nor any other creature will be able to separate us from the love of God that comes to us in Christ, Jesus, our Lord." (8:38–39)

And beyond the body, beyond story, beyond the workings of the mind, are the visions of Revelation, assuring us that after death there will be no more mourning, sadness, or pain. "He shall wipe every tear from their eyes.... The One who sat on the throne said to me, 'See I, make all thing new.... I am the Alpha and the Omega, the Beginning and the End. To anyone who thirsts I will give to drink without cost from the spring of life-giving water. He who wins the victory shall inherit these gifts; I will be his God and he shall be my son.' " (21:4–7)

What is promised, after all, can only be won by walking through the gates of death: The vision of glory where the meaning of suffering will either be revealed or, perhaps, seem of no consequence.

It takes the polyphony of all these voices to contain the whole meaning of the sacrament of the Anointing of the Sick. Because the task of the sacrament is complex, it sacralizes the transition between life and death, but it does not pass over the transition without an acknowledgment of its crucial significance. It insists that we acknowledge that the failures of the body are an inevitable part of its history, a part from which we must not avert our eyes. Nor must we banish or hide those who remind us of our own inevitable fate; we must praise their witness; we must offer them comfort and hope. We must be with them in all the aspects of their experience that the various scriptural readings invoke: dread, aloneness, anger, loss of faith. But we must understand that this is not the whole or the end of the story; there is, as well, hope for accompaniment, vision of a future without a body, a future of unapproachable light.

The word *community* has become so debased and so misused that we forget that it has the possibilities in it of transcendence. The Church is and must be a community of the living; if it doesn't provide something that nothing else can provide, there's not much sense to the enormous material and psychic costs of keeping it up. The sacrament of Anointing touches that part of the broken body that doctors, social workers, and loving family and friends cannot approach: the part that, in order to be healed, must acknowledge its despair and travel from it to a place of hope. And this is what a sacrament must be: a vehicle for the journey between the seen and the unseen.

SOURCES

Robert Hovda, *The Amen Corner* (Collegeville, MN: Pueblo, 1994).

Aidan Kavanagh, *On Liturgical Theology* (Collegeville, MN: Pueblo, 1992).

————, *The Shape of Baptism: The Rite of Christian Initiation* (Collegeville, MN: Liturgical Press, 1978).

Richard P. McBrien, *Catholicism* (Minneapolis: Winston, 1981).

————, editor, *The HarperCollins Encyclopedia of Catholicism* (San Francisco: Harper San Francisco, 1995).

Pastoral Care of the Sick: Rites of Anointing and Viaticum (New York: Catholic Book Publishing Co., 1983).

Simone Weil, *Waiting for God* (New York: Harper & Row, 1973).

EPILOGUE:
SACRAMENTS

ANDRE DUBUS

A sacrament is physical, and within it is God's love; as a sandwich is physical, and nutritious and pleasurable, and within it is love, if someone makes it for you and gives it to you with love—even harried or tired or impatient love, but with love's direction and concern, love's again and again wavering and distorted focus on goodness; then God's love too is in the sandwich. A sacrament is an outward sign of God's love, they taught me when I was a boy, and in the Catholic church there are seven. But, no, I say, for the Church is catholic, the world is catholic, and there are seven times seventy sacraments, to infinity. Today I sit at my desk in June in Massachusetts; a breeze from the southeast comes through the window behind me, touches me, and goes through the open glass door in front of me. The sky is blue, and cumulus clouds are motionless above green trees lit brightly by the sun shining in dry air. In humid air the leaves would be darker, but now they are bright, and you can see lighted space between them, so that each leaf is distinct; and each leaf is receiving sacraments of light and air and water and earth. So am I, in the breeze on my skin, the air I breathe, the sky and earth and trees I look at.

Sacraments are myriad. It is good to be baptized, to confess and be reconciled, to receive Communion, to be confirmed, to be ordained a priest, to marry, or to be anointed with the sacrament of healing. But it is limiting to believe that sacraments occur only in churches, or when someone comes to us in a hospital or at home and anoints our brows and eyes and ears, our noses and lips, hearts and hands and feet. I try to receive Communion daily, but I never go to Mass day after day after day, because I cannot sleep when I want to, I take pills, and if the pills allow me to sleep before midnight, I usually can wake up at 7:30 and do what I must to get to Mass. But I know that when I do not go to Mass, I am still receiving Communion, because I desire it; and because God is in me, as he is in the light, the earth, the leaf. I only have to lie on my bed, waking after Mass has already ended, and I am receiving sacraments with each breath, as I did while I slept; with each movement of my body as I exercise my lower abdomen to ease the pain in my back caused by sitting for fifteen hours: in my wheelchair, my car, and on my couch, before going to bed for the night; receiving sacraments as I perform crunches and leg lifts, then dress and make the bed while sitting on it. Being at Mass and receiving Communion give me joy and strength. Receiving Communion of desire on my bed does not, for I cannot feel joy with my brain alone. I need sacraments I can receive through my senses. I need God manifested as Christ, who ate and drank and shat and suffered, and laughed. So I can dance with Him as the leaf dances in the breeze under the sun.

Not remembering that we are always receiving sacraments is an isolation the leaves do not have to endure: they receive and give, and they are green. Not remembering this is an isolation only the human soul has to endure. But the isolation of a human soul may be the cause of not remembering this. Between isolation and harmony, there is not always a vast distance. Sometimes it is a distance that can be traversed in a moment, by choosing to focus on the essence of what is occurring, rather than on its exterior: its difficulty or beauty, its demands or joy, peace or grief, passion or humor. This is not a matter of courage or discipline or will; it is a receptive condition.

Because I am divorced, on Tuesdays I drive to my daughters' school, where they are in the seventh and second grades. I have them with me on other days, and some nights, but Tuesday is the school day. They do not like the food at their school, and the school does not allow them to bring food, so after classes they are hungry, and I bring them sandwiches, potato chips, Cokes, Reese's peanut butter cups. My kitchen is very small; if one person is standing in it, I cannot make a three-hundred-and-sixty-degree turn. When I roll into the kitchen to make the girls' sandwiches, if I remember to stop at the first set of drawers on my right, just inside the door, and get plastic bags and write *Cadence* on one and *Madeleine* on the other, then stop at the second set of drawers and get three knives for spreading mayonnaise and mustard and cutting the sandwiches in half, then turn sharply left and reach over the sink for the cutting board leaning upright behind the faucet, then put all these things on the counter to my right, beside the refrigerator, and bend forward and reach into the refrigerator for the meat and cheese and mustard and mayonnaise, and reach up into the freezer for bread, I can do all of this with one turn of the chair. This is a First World problem; I ought to be only grateful. Sometimes I remember this, and then I believe that most biped fathers in the world would exchange their legs for my wheelchair and house and food, medical insurance and my daughters' school.

Making sandwiches while sitting in a wheelchair is not physically difficult. But it can be a spiritual trial; the chair always makes me remember my legs, and how I lived with them. I am beginning my ninth year as a cripple, and have learned to try to move slowly, with concentration, with precision, with peace. Forgetting plastic bags in the first set of drawers and having to turn the chair around to get them is nothing. The memory of having legs that held me upright at this counter and the image of simply turning from the counter and stepping to the drawer are the demons I must keep at bay, or I will rage and grieve because of space, and time, and this wheeled thing that has replaced my legs. So I must try to know the spiritual essence of what I am doing.

On Tuesdays when I make lunches for my girls, I focus on this: the sandwiches are sacraments. Not the miracle of transubstantiation, but certainly parallel with it, moving in the same direction. If I could give my children my body to eat, again and again without losing it, my body like the loaves and fishes going endlessly into mouths and stomachs, I would do it. And each motion is a sacrament, this holding of plastic bags, of knives, of bread, of cutting board, this pushing of the chair, this spreading of mustard on bread, this trimming of liverwurst, of ham. All sacraments, as putting the lunches into a zippered book bag is, and going down my six ramps to my car is. I drive on the highway, to the girls' town, to their school, and this is not simply a transition; it is my love moving by car from a place where my girls are not to a place where they are; even if I do not feel or acknowledge it, this is a sacrament. If I remember it, then I feel it too. Feeling it does not always mean that I am a happy man driving in traffic; it simply means that I know what I am doing in the presence of God.

If I were much wiser, and much more patient, and had much greater concentration, I could sit in silence in my chair, look out my windows at a green tree and the blue sky, and know that breathing is a gift; that a breath is efficient for the moment; and that breathing air is breathing God.

You can receive and give sacraments with a telephone. In a very lonely time, two years after my crippling, I met a woman with dark skin and black hair and wit and verbal grace. We were together for an autumn afternoon, and I liked her, and that evening I sat on my couch with her, and held and kissed her. Then she drove three and a half hours north to her home in Vermont. I had a car then, with hand controls, but I had not learned to drive it; my soul was not ready for the tension and fear. I did not see the woman until five weeks later. I courted her by telephone, daily or nightly or both. She agreed to visit me and my family at

Thanksgiving. On Halloween I had a heart attack, and courted her with the bedside telephone in the hospital. Once after midnight, while I was talking to her, a nurse came into the room, smiled at me, and took the clipboard from the foot of the bed and wrote what she saw. Next morning, in my wheelchair, I read: *Twelve-fifteen. Patient alert and cheerful, talking on the phone.*

In the five weeks since that sunlit October day when I first saw her, I knew this woman through her voice. Then on Thanksgiving she drove to a motel in the town where I live, and in early afternoon came to my house for dinner with my family: my first wife and our four grown children, and one daughter's boyfriend and one son's girlfriend, and my two young daughters. That night, when the family left, she stayed and made love to my crippled body, which did not feel crippled with her, save for some pain in my leg. Making love can be a sacrament, if our souls are as naked as our bodies, if our souls are in harmony with our bodies, and through our bodies are embracing each other in love and fear and trembling, knowing that this act could be the beginning of a third human being, if we are a man and a woman; knowing that the roots and trunk of death are within each of us, and that one of its branches may block or rupture an artery as we kiss. Surely this is a sacrament, as it may not be if we are with someone whose arms we would not want holding us as, suddenly, in passion, we died; someone whose death in our arms would pierce us not with grief but regret, fear, shame; someone who would not want to give life to that third person who is always present in lovemaking between fertile men and women. On the day after

Thanksgiving she checked out of the motel and stayed with me until Monday and I loved her; then she went home.

She came to me on other weekends, four to six weeks apart, and we loved each other daily by telephone. That winter she moved to New York City. I still did not drive, and her apartment was not a place I could enter and be in with my wheelchair; it was very small, and so was the shared bathroom down the hall. I could not fly to her, because my right knee does not bend, so I have to sit on the first seat of an airplane, and that means a first-class ticket. Trains are inaccessible horrors for someone in a wheelchair: the aisles are too narrow. A weekend in New York, if I flew there and stayed in a hotel, would have cost over a thousand dollars, before we bought a drink or a meal. So she flew to Boston or rode on the train, and a friend drove me to meet her. I was a virtual shut-in who was in love. One day a week, my oldest son drove me to horseback riding lessons; in the barn, he pushed me up a ramp to a platform level with the horse's back, and I mounted and rode, guarded from falling by my son and volunteer women who walked and jogged beside me. A driver of a wheelchair van came for me two mornings a week and took me to Mass and left, then came back and took me to physical therapy, then came back and took me home, where I lay on my bed and held the telephone and talked to the woman, sometimes more than once a day. With the telephone she gave me sacraments I needed during that fall and winter when my body seemed to be my enemy. We were lovers for a year, and then we were not, and now our love remains and sharing our flesh is no longer essential.

On the night of Christmas Eve, in that year when we were

lovers, I was very sad and I called her. The Christmas tree was in the living room, tall and full, and from the kitchen doorway, where I held the telephone, I could see in the front windows the reflection of the tree and its ornaments and lights. My young daughters' stockings were hanging at the windows, but my girls were at their mother's house, and would wake there Christmas morning, and would come to me in the afternoon. I was a crippled father in an empty house. In my life, I have been too much a father in an empty house; and since the vocation of fatherhood includes living with the mother, this is the deepest shame of my life, and its abiding regret. I sat in my chair and spoke into the phone of the pain in my soul, and she listened, and talked to me, and finally said: "You're supposed to be happy. It's your hero's birthday."

I laughed with my whole heart at the humor of it, at the truth of it, and now my pain was bearable, my sorrow not a well but drops of water drying in the winter room.

In March I decided one day that I must stop talking to her on the telephone because, while I did, I was amused, interested, passionate, joyful; then I said good-bye and I was a cripple who had been sitting in his wheelchair or lying on his bed, holding plastic to his ear. I told her that if I were whole, and could hang up the telephone and walk out of the house, I would not stop calling her; but I knew that living this way, receiving her by telephone, was not a good crippled way to live; and I knew there was a better crippled way to live, but I did not know yet what it was. She understood; she always does, whether or not she agrees.

I did not call her for days and on the first day of April, I woke crying, and on the second; and on the third I could not stop, and I phoned my doctor's receptionist and, still crying, I told her to tell him to give me a shot or put me away someplace, because I could not bear it anymore. At noon he brought me spinach pie and chili dogs, and I said: "That's cholesterol."

"Depression will kill you sooner," he said, and I ate with him and still did not understand that the food and his presence at my table were sacraments. He made an appointment for me with a psychologist, and two days later my youngest son drove me to the office of this paternal and compassionate man, who said: "This is not depression; it's sorrow, and it'll always be with you, because you can't replace your legs."

As my son drove me home, I told him that I wanted a swimming pool, but I did not want to be a man who needed a swimming pool to be happy. He said: "You're not asking the world for a swimming pool. You're asking it for motion."

At home, I called a paraplegic friend and asked him to teach me to drive my car, and two days later he did. I phoned a swimming pool contractor, a durably merry and kind man, and his cost for building me a forty-by-fifteen-by-three-foot lap pool was so generous that I attribute it to gimpathy. Sacraments abounded. I paid for some, and the money itself was sacramental: my being alive to receive it and give it for good work. On that first day, after calling the paraplegic and the contractor, I called the woman, and I continued to call her, and to receive that grace.

On the last day of my father's life, he was thirsty and he asked me to crush some ice, and feed it to him. I was a marine captain, stationed at Whidbey Island, Washington, and I had flown home to Lake Charles, Louisiana, to be with my father before he died, and when he died, and to bury him. I did not know then that the night flight from Seattle was more than a movement in air from my wife and four young children to my dying father, that every moment of it, even as I slept, was a sacrament I gave my father; and they were sacraments he gave me, his siring and his love drawing me to him through the night; and sacraments between my mother and two sisters and me, and all the relatives and friends I was flying home to; and my wife and children and me, for their love was with me on the plane and I loved them and I would return to them after burying my father; and from Time itself, God's mystery we often do not clearly see; there was time now to be with my father. Sacraments came from those who flew the plane and worked aboard it and maintained it and controlled its comings and goings; and from the major who gave me emergency leave, and the gunnery sergeant who did my work while I was gone. I did not know any of this. I thought I was a son flying alone.

My father's cancer had begun in his colon, and on the Saturday before the early Sunday morning when he died, it was consuming him, and he was thin and weak on his bed, and he asked for ice. In the kitchen, I emptied a tray of ice cubes onto a dish towel and held its four corners and twisted it, then held it on the counter and with a rolling pin pounded the ice till it was crushed. This is how my father crushed ice, and how my sisters and I, when we were children, crushed it and put it in a glass and spooned sugar on it, to eat on a hot summer day. I put my father's ice into a tall glass and brought it with an iced tea spoon to the bedroom and fed him the ice, one small piece at a time, until his mouth and throat were no longer dry.

As a boy I was shy with my father. Perhaps he was shy with me too. When we were alone in a car, we were mostly silent. On some nights, when a championship boxing match was broadcast on the radio, we listened to it in the living room. He took me to wrestling matches because I wanted to go, and he told me they were fake, and I refused to believe it. He took me to minor league baseball games. While we listened to boxing matches and watched wrestling and baseball, we talked about what we were hearing and seeing. He took me fishing and dove hunting with his friends, before I was old enough to shoot; but I could fish from the bank of a bayou, and he taught me to shoot my air rifle; taught me so well that, years later, my instructors in the Marine Corps simply polished his work. When I was still too young to use a shotgun, he learned to play golf and stopped fishing and hunting, and on Saturdays and Sundays he brought me to the golf course as his caddy. I did not want to caddy, but I had no choice, and I earned a dollar and a quarter; all my adult life, I have been grateful that I watched him and listened to him with his friends, and talked with him about his game. My shyness with him was a burden I did not like carrying, and I could not put down. Then I was twenty-one and a husband and a marine, and on the morning my pregnant wife and I left home, to drive to the Officers' Basic School in Quantico, Virginia, my father and I tightly embraced, then looked at each other's damp eyes. I wanted to say *I love you*, but I could not.

I wanted to say it to him before he died. In the afternoon of his last day, he wanted bourbon and water. A lot of ice, he told me, and a lot of water. I made drinks for my sister and me too, and brought his in a tall glass I did not hold for him. I do not remember whether he lifted it to his mouth or rested it on his chest and drank from an angled hospital straw. My sister and I sat in chairs at the foot of the bed, my mother talked with relatives and friends in the living room and brought them in to speak to my father, and I told him stories of my year of sea duty on an aircraft carrier, of my work at Whidbey Island. Once he asked me to light him a cigarette. I went to his bedside table, put one of his cigarettes between my lips, lit his Zippo, then looked beyond the cigarette and flame at my father's eyes: they were watching me. All my life at home before I left for the Marine Corps, I had felt him watching me, a glance during a meal or in the living room or on the lawn, had felt he was trying to see my soul, to see if I were strong and honorable, to see if I could go out into the world, and live in it without him. His eyes watching me light his cigarette were tender, and they were saying good-bye.

That night my father's sisters slept in the beds that had been mine and my sister's, and she and I went to the house of a neighbor across the street. We did not sleep. We sat in the kitchen and drank and cried, and I told her that tomorrow I would tell my father I loved him. Before dawn he died, and for years I regretted not saying the words. But I did not understand love then, and the sacraments that make it tactile. I had not lived enough and lost enough to enable me to know the holiness of working with meat and mustard and bread; of moving on wheels or wings or by foot from one place to another; of holding a telephone and speaking into it and listening to a voice; of pounding ice with wood and spooning the shards onto a dry tongue; of lighting a cigarette and placing it between the fingers of a man trying to enjoy tobacco and bourbon and his family as he dies.

ABOUT THE
CONTRIBUTORS

MURRAY BODO, O.F.M., is writer-in-residence at Thomas More College in Crestview Hills, Kentucky. A member of the Franciscan Academy, Father Murray has spent fifteen summers in Umbria on the staff of Franciscan Pilgrimage Programs, leading pilgrims in the footsteps of Saint Francis. He is the author of fifteen books, including, *Francis: The Journey and the Dream* (1988). His latest work is a double audio cassette from Sounds True, entitled, *The Way of St. Francis: Teachings and Practices for Daily Life.*

ANDRE DUBUS, who was born in Lake Charles, Louisiana, was the author of several works of fiction, including *Adultery and Other Choices* (1981), *The Times Are Never So Bad* (1983), *Voices from the Moon* (1984), *The Last Worthless Evening* (1987), *Selected Stories* (1996), and *Dancing After Hours* (1996). Dubus received the PEN/Malamud Award, the Rea Award for excellence in short fiction, the Jean Stein Award from the American Academy of Arts and Letters, and fellowships from both the Guggenheim and MacArthur Foundations. *Meditations from a Movable Chair*, his final collection of essays, was published in May 1998. He died on February 25, 1999, in Haverhill, Massachusetts.

MARY GORDON is the author of many highly acclaimed novels, including *Final Payments* (1978), *The Company of Women* (1980), *Men and Angels* (1985), *The Other Side* (1989), and most recently *Spending* (1998). She has also published a book of novellas, *The Rest of Life* (1993); a collection of stories, *Temporary Shelter* (1987); and a book of essays, *Good Boys and Dead Girls* (1991). Her critically acclaimed memoir of her father, *The Shadow Man*, was published in 1996. Gordon has received the Lila Acheson Wallace–Reader's Digest Writer's Award, a Guggenheim Fellowship, and the 1996 O. Henry Prize for best short story. She is a professor of English at Barnard College.

PATRICIA HAMPL's most recent book is *I Could Tell You Stories: Sojourns in the Land of Memory* (1999). Her other books include *Virgin Time* (1992), a memoir about her Catholic upbringing and an inquiry into contemplative life, and *A Romantic Education* (1981), about her Czech heritage, reissued in 1999 with a new Afterword in honor of the tenth anniversary of the Velvet Revolution. She has also published two volumes of poetry, *Woman Before an Aquarium* (1978) and *Resort and Other Poems* (1983), as well as *Spillville* (1987), a prose meditation on Antonin Dvorak's 1893 stay in Iowa. She is the editor of *The Houghton Mifflin Anthology of Short Fiction* (1989) and of *Burning Bright* (1995), an anthology of sacred poems from Judaism, Christianity, and Islam. Her fiction has appeared in *The Best American Short Stories* series and the *Pushcart Prize Anthology*, and an essay will appear in the next *Best American Essays* anthology. Her last three books have been *New York Times* "Notable Books of the Year." Hampl is Regents' Professor at the University of Minnesota where she teaches in the MFA program of the Department of English. She is also on the permanent faculty of the Prague Summer Seminars.

RON HANSEN is the author of several works of fiction, including *Atticus* (1995), *Mariette in Ecstasy* (1990), *The Assassination of Jesse James by the Coward Robert Ford* (1983), *Desperadoes* (1979), and most recently *Hitler's Niece* (1999). He is also the editor, with Jim Shepard, of *You've Got to Read This: Contemporary American Writers Introduce Stories That Held Them in Awe* (1994). Hansen has held the Wallace Stegner Creative Writing Fellowship at Stanford, has twice been nominated for a PEN/Faulkner Award, was a finalist for the National Book Award for *Atticus*, and a recipient of an Award in Literature from the American Academy and Institute of Arts and Letters. He is the Gerard Manley Hopkins, S.J., Professor in Arts and Humanities at Santa Clara University, where he earned an M.A. in Spirituality in 1995.

PAULA HUSTON's short fiction has appeared in numerous literary journals; her first novel, *Daughters of Song*, was published in 1995.

She is currently revising a second novel and a collection of short stories, and is working on a new book of essays about her solo trip around the world. A National Endowment for the Arts Fellow, she teaches fiction writing and literature at Cal Poly San Luis Obispo and in the California State University Consortium Master of Fine Arts degree program.

PAUL MARIANI is the author of four widely acclaimed biographies: *William Carlos Williams: A New World Naked* (1981), a finalist for the National Book Award; *Dream Song: The Life of John Berryman* (1990, rev. 1995); *Lost Puritan: A Life of Robert Lowell* (1995); and *The Broken Tower: A Life of Hart Crane* (1999). He is also the author of book-length commentaries on Hopkins and Williams; five volumes of poetry, including *Salvage Operations* (1990) and *The Great Wheel* (1996); a book of essays on modern and contemporary poetry; and hundreds of reviews and articles, many on the religious and theological implications of modern literature. He has taught modern and contemporary poetry at the University of Massachusetts for the last thirty years, where he is Distinguished University Professor.

KATHERINE VAZ's novels include *Saudade* (1994), in English and Portuguese, a selection of the Barnes & Noble Discover Great New Writers series, and *Mariana* (1997), in English, German, Italian, Spanish, Portuguese, and Greek, with film rights optioned by Harrison Productions. *Fado & Other Stories* won the 1997 Drue Heinz Literature Prize. Her short fiction has appeared in numerous literary quarterlies, and her nonfiction has been published in *The New York Times* and *The Boston Globe*. She is a recipient of a National Endowment for the Arts Fellowship and is the first Portuguese American to have her work recorded for the Hispanic Division of the U.S. Library of Congress.